Praise for Marianne Williamson's
A Return to Love

"Marianne Williamson's book is a classic. She reveals, with elegant simplicity, that love is not a mere sentiment of emotion, but the ultimate truth at the heart of creation."
—Deepak Chopra, MD

"With this gutsy book Marianne Williamson has single-handedly ushered in a powerful spiritual renewal. I wholeheartedly recommend your reading it."
—John Bradshaw, author of *Homecoming: Reclaiming and Championing Your Inner Child* and *Creating Love: The Next Great Stage of Growth*

"Using humorous personal narrative, Williamson explains how applying love to all difficulties, as advised by *The Course*, can aid in healing."
—*Library Journal*

"When I first read *A Return to Love*, I literally felt the excitement as I absorbed Marianne Williamson's insights. Today, it is still a treasure to me, and Marianne is a light for the transformation of the world. You will love this book. I guarantee it."
—Wayne Dyer, author of the Law of Attraction series and *Real Magic*

THE
MYSTIC
JESUS

ALSO BY MARIANNE WILLIAMSON

A Return to Love

The Gift of Change

A Year of Miracles

The Law of Divine Compensation

Tears to Triumph

A Politics of Love

MARIANNE WILLIAMSON

THE
MYSTIC
JESUS

THE MIND OF LOVE

HarperOne
An Imprint of HarperCollins*Publishers*

HarperCollins books may be purchased for educational, business, or sales promotional use. For information, please email the Special Markets Department at SPsales@harpercollins.com.

Art by Ermak Oksana/Shutterstock, Inc.

FIRST EDITION

Library of Congress Cataloging-in-Publication Data is available upon request.

ISBN 978-0-06-220547-6

24 25 26 27 28 LBC 5 4 3 2 1

To Mickey Maudlin,
for quiet guidance and the opportunity of a lifetime.

You are a perfect creation, and should experience awe only in the Presence of the Creator of perfection. ⁴The miracle is therefore a sign of love among equals. ⁵Equals should not be in awe of one another because awe implies inequality. ⁶It is therefore an inappropriate reaction to me. ⁷An elder brother is entitled to respect for his greater experience, and obedience for his greater wisdom. ⁸He is also entitled to love because he is a brother, and to devotion if he is devoted. ⁹It is only my devotion that entitles me to yours. ¹⁰There is nothing about me that you cannot attain. ¹¹I have nothing that does not come from God. ¹²The difference between us now is that I have nothing else. ¹³This leaves me in a state which is only potential in you. (A Course in Miracles, Text, 7)

CONTENTS

PREFACE

I AM NOT A Christian scholar, nor am I a Christian. I would not be qualified, therefore, to write about the Jesus espoused by the ecclesiastic traditions of the Christian church.

Rather, this book is based on my more than four decades as a student of *A Course in Miracles*. The *Course* is a self-study program of spiritual psychotherapy based on universal spiritual themes, employing traditional Christian concepts expressed in nondogmatic, psychotherapeutic ways. It is a psychological training in the relinquishment of a thought system based on fear in favor of a thought system based on love.

I was a young woman in my twenties when I first picked up *A Course in Miracles*, searching for meaning and purpose in my life, no different from anyone at that age then or now. I was intrigued by these words in its introduction:

> *The Course can therefore be summed*
> *up very simply in this way:*
> **Nothing real can be threatened.**
> **Nothing unreal exists.**
> *Herein lies the peace of God.*

Though I found those words compelling, I saw the pages of the book were filled with traditional Christian language. I didn't relate to the *Course*'s terminology and simply thought it wasn't for me.

A year later I was in such emotional turmoil that the terminology in a book didn't matter to me, and I picked it up again. I was looking for content that would soothe my soul and I didn't care what the words were. This wasn't about theology, it was about my life.

It quickly became clear that the *Course* is not a religion but only psychological guidance in the ways of forgiveness and love. I had always been interested in universal spiritual concepts, sensing there is one Truth spoken in many different ways. Many of the universal themes contained in the *Course* I had encountered elsewhere, including in my own religion, Judaism. But what the *Course* had offered me that I hadn't found before were practical ways to apply these concepts to my daily life.

From the beginning I was bemused by the fact that no author was named on the cover of *A Course in Miracles*. The more I read it, however, the more I saw an interesting number of statements written in the first person.

"'No man cometh unto the Father but by me' does not mean that I am in any way separate or different from you except in time"* (T-2). I remember reading that and thinking, *Wait, what?* Once I read "I am the Atonement"* (T-7), I was like, *Okay, I get it.*

As a child I never heard much about Jesus one way or the other. I was just told we read "the other Bible." For Jews, there is a distinct difference between a reaction to Jesus and a reaction to Christian-

---

* Throughout this book, when I am directly stating a concept from *A Course in Miracles*, the sentence will be followed by an asterisk (*). Direct quotations will be identified as coming from its Text (T), Workbook (WB), Psychotherapy: Purpose, Process, and Practice (P), or Manual for Teachers (MT).

ity, which should come as a surprise to no one. Jesus was a Jew; he was one of us. Institutional forces within the Christian religion, on the other hand, have often been a source of violent antisemitism and murderous oppression through millennia.

None of that has anything to do with Jesus, however. Christianity and Jesus are two distinctly different things. At times, the Christian religion has been known to uphold the highest ideals of Jesus, while at other times and places it decidedly has not. At times, as it says in the *Course*, "some bitter idols have been made of him who came only to be brother to the world"* (MT-88).

My interest in Jesus has never included a desire to convert to the Christian religion, a fact natural enough to me but that had required an explanation to my parents. When I first became a student of the *Course*, they were understandably perplexed. I remember my mother saying to me haltingly, "So, help me understand. You're going to stay in California... and give talks... about Jesus... to *Gentiles*!?" I slowly nodded. After a few seconds she simply shook her head, raised an eyebrow, and asked me what I was going to wear.

My father seemed more concerned. One day he took me aside and said very intently, "It's the *same God*, isn't it?"

I said, "Yes, Daddy! Of course it is!"

I remember his looking at me sternly and saying pointedly, "Okay, I just don't want to hear anything about a different God."

No, it's decidedly not a different God! Permission granted.

As I read the *Course*, I found the concepts so fascinating that I naively assumed my Christian friends must sit around and talk about things like Christ, the Holy Spirit, and Jesus all the time. I figured I just didn't know that because they didn't do it when I was in the room! Silly me. What I came to realize was something quite different. Many Christians I knew had even more aversion to all that Christian terminology than I had had. I was simply ignorant of certain concepts; they were ambivalent about them.

The *Course* frees Jesus from the grip of an institutional authority that seeks to monopolize and ultimately constrict his identity. For some the *Course* deviates from Christian principles, while for others it explains them in a way that makes sense for the first time. As it says in the *Course*, its practitioners come from "all religions and no religion." They are simply those who have heard the call for a higher, transformative love.

I learned that many Christians as well as non-Christians are filled with a lot of questions about Jesus. Reading the *Course*, I was learning some new ideas, while some of my friends were unlearning old ones. I have seen thousands of people over the years, both Christian and non-Christian, find profound psychological and spiritual value in *A Course in Miracles*. The mystic Jesus is reflective of themes at the heart of all the great religions of the world. He is not a divider into religious silos but rather a connector of human hearts.

A Course in Miracles does not ask us to believe in God, or in Jesus. It asks us to believe in each other. It argues that belief itself is meaningless, but that experience is everything. Some believe *A Course in Miracles* is a work of genius created by a clinical psychology professor named Helen Schucman at Columbia University in the 1960s and 1970s, while others believe it was written by the Holy Spirit speaking through her. The power of the *Course* is expressed not through the identification of its author but in the practice of its principles.

I feel grateful that I came to the *Course* with no previous understanding of who Jesus was or is. My mind was devoid of preconceived notions, and at no point during my more than four decades of studying it have I felt called away from my own religion. What the *Course* is asking us to convert is our hearts, and that is all. If anything, my study of *A Course in Miracles* has connected me more deeply to the mystical roots of Judaism.

This book is about the Jesus I know as a student of *A Course in Miracles*. All the concepts you will read here are based on my understanding of his teachings. Everyone has their own experience of *A Course in Miracles* and of its author. This is simply mine.

INTRODUCTION

MANY YEARS AGO, I went through a painful ordeal. It was a very rough period of my life.

During that time I had an odd experience. As I lay awake night after night unable to sleep, I began to sense a strange energy—a shadowy presence like that of a very thin, tall man, sitting upright at the end of my bed perpendicular to how I was lying. He was simply there. Not doing anything. Not looking at me. Just there.

I had been a student of *A Course in Miracles* for a while at that point, and I was familiar with feeling God's presence. But I hadn't had any specific sense of relationship to Jesus. Now, seeing this figure at the end of my bed, I began to wonder...

During that period I knew I was in trouble psychologically; I could see it on the faces of my family and friends when they looked at me. I experienced what today would be called a nervous breakdown.

I didn't realize it at the time, but what I was going through was something that most people feel to some extent, but which many have grown adept at covering over. The gap between the world we're living in and the world our hearts are calling for is growing into an increasingly unsustainable stress point. Today, almost forty years later, we are living a life so at odds with who we are. Cracking under the strain of it all feels more like the rule than the exception. Our society calls it a mental health crisis, but in fact it's a spiritual one. There is a profound disconnection between the love in our hearts and how we are living on the earth.

The truth of our being is not reflected in the world we see around us, so much as it is contradicted, obscured, and even violated by the world. The realities of the modern world do more to bruise than to heal the wounded soul, and the purpose of our lives is to repair the damage.

My mother didn't know what to do with a daughter who couldn't stop crying, and she told me she would send me to therapy. "My friend Buzz says you need to see someone," she said.

I responded, "Ya think?"

"But none of that crazy California stuff you do!" she said. (I had been living in New York, but my mother labeled anything nontraditional "California.") "I want it to be a medical doctor. A Jewish psychiatrist."

Fine, Mom, I thought, *just try to help me, please.* And when I walked into the psychiatrist's office, one of the first things I said to him was "Look, I'm a student of a set of books called *A Course in Miracles*, and you need to know that. If you're going to tell me that's crazy and delusional and what I need is serious psychiatric help but that's not it, then this isn't going to work."

To my amazement and eternal gratitude, he leaned over in his chair and said, "I just finished the Workbook." He was a student of *A Course in Miracles*.

It was during that time that I felt the presence at the end of my bed. And it was also during that time that I proposed a kind of deal to God. In a moment of despair, I told Him that if He would help me put my life back together, then I would dedicate the rest of it to Him.

Slowly but surely, and with the help of that amazing psychiatrist in Houston, I healed. I felt as though my head had exploded into thousands of little pieces, sending shards of my skull out into the outer regions of the universe. It took time, but when my skull came back together it felt like something had entered my brain that hadn't been there before. My perceptual framework was somehow rearranged.

As the months passed, I forgot about that moment when I had proposed a deal to God. In fact, I started feeling like my old self again. I didn't sense a presence at the end of my bed anymore, but I still felt *something* that I couldn't quite put my finger on. It was as though I had been accompanied in my grief. Now, however, what had felt so comforting before began to feel kind of weird. What had felt like a reassuring presence began to feel like a bit of an intrusion as I was going about my day.

In fact, I tried to shoo it away.

"Look, I'm extremely grateful to you. But I'm fine now, really. I'm sure you have many, many other people to help, and I think you should go do that! Thanks so much. Really. Bye-bye!"

I was trying to blow off Jesus.

Then not long afterward, an interesting thing happened at a cocktail party I attended in Houston. The party was at a big house filled with smaller rooms. The party sort of floated from one room to the next.

At one point I entered a room and saw about three or four men dressed in tuxedos, drinks in hand, standing around talking to each other. And in what must have been a waking dream—ancients would have called it a mystical experience, perhaps—one of the men turned his head and looked at me. In that moment, I gasped. For I knew who he was.

He simply looked at me, saying without any emotion whatsoever, "I thought we had a deal."

And that was it.

I have found over the years that I'm far from alone in having had a strange introduction to Jesus. The prepackaged religious Jesus doesn't work for everyone, including some Christians. For many he has become like a fossil enclosed within a glass case, displayed in a museum but somehow lacking spiritual force.

The world needs help—few are doubting that now—but religious dogma seems like an inadequate response to the challenges of our time. People long for a sense of spiritual immediacy, not some promise of a vague and far-off heaven. Nothing narrow, rigid, or inauthentic grabs the modern soul. If there's something that bears witness to our horror at the pain of living, that speaks to our yearning to escape the trauma of simply being in this world, and delivers us to realistic hope that things could actually get better, then we're definitely open. But not to stultified notions of an otherworldly benefactor who stands by while humanity suffers. Nope. Too late for that. There's a sense among millions that that might have worked for others at another time, but it won't work for us.

In turning away from the dogma of organized religion, however, people don't necessarily mean to be turning away from God. Many are scanning the landscape now for new, more vital spiritual experiences, including a revelation of Jesus that is more relevant to their lives. They're finding this revelation both inside *and* outside the Christian religion. Surely there's something beyond the false choice between a calcified notion of a "Son of

God" and the modern de-juiced assignation of "a great teacher." We're looking for a deliverer not just from our individual sins but from the world's insanity. And nothing less will do.

We understand that the problems of our world cry out for something deeper than either the shallowness of institutional religion or the bromides of popular culture. The quest for that something deeper relates to every collective challenge we face now, and people know it. This book is an exploration of the role of Jesus in helping us find what that is.

Just as Jesus two thousand years ago came to speak not only to Jews, the Jesus of today comes to speak not only to Christians. The idea that he belongs only to Christians, or to practitioners of any other religion, for that matter—who therefore get to determine precisely who he is and what he should mean to us—is an idea whose time is passing. While Christianity claims a kind of monopoly on Jesus, there's a growing sense that he belongs to no one and yet to everyone.

The mystic Jesus is a universal Jesus, an aspect of nature itself. I experience the sun, but no one owns the sun. I experience the breeze, but no one owns the breeze. I experience love, but no one owns love. Natural forces can neither be contained nor propertied, and Jesus is a natural force.

The mystic Jesus is a path of consciousness, an understanding of how the universe operates and how we can mentally align with its purposes. The contemporary mystic is guided by an internal radar that exists within us all, literally a gift from God. Whether we call that guidance conscience, ethics, our covenant with God, the voice of the Holy Spirit, or Jesus, its wisdom and illumination is the salvation of the world.

When Jesus said, "My kingdom is not of this world," that is what he was referring to—that his kingdom is not an outer but rather an inner domain of existence, what today we call the psyche. His is a mindset of love, which he shares with us when we ask him to. The only thing to be saved from is our own misguided belief that we are separate and alone in a random and meaningless universe—for that is the source of all fear. The reason Jesus can be called savior of the world is because he saves us from our sick thinking about the world. Jesus is a guide to another way of thinking—thus the builder of another kind of world.

The world is a reflection of our thoughts; therefore the primary thing to be saved from is our own misguided thinking. The salvation of the world lies in the correction of the thinking that dominates this world, a kind of thinking that is rooted in fear and leads inevitably to fearsome consequences. The problems of the world as we know them are simply symptoms of a deeper problem: *us*, and the ways of thinking that trap us in the hell of our own making. It is thinking based on fear, positing us as separate from everything—from anything larger than ourselves, from each other, and from the world at large. This thinking is deeply untrue and deeply insane. It wounds the world because it breaks the heart. It causes inevitable suffering because it is so at odds with the truth of who we are. We need to correct that thinking, and then we will correct the world. We need to heal our wounded souls, and then we will heal the world.

It is imperative that we stop behaving in ways so violently destructive to ourselves and to others and to the planet on which we live, or humanity will not survive itself. Our violent behavior stems from our violent thinking; it is our thinking, therefore, that is killing us. Yet how do we change at this point? Is anyone seriously thinking that traditional psychotherapy, or psychopharmacology, or theology is going to save us? "A universal theology is impossible, but a universal experience is not only possible but necessary"* (MT-77), says the *Course*.

And what is that experience? What is the shift in thinking that will lead to a change in behavior that will lead to a different kind of world? The spiritual path is simply the journey of the heart, and as the world embarks on that journey then our world is going to change.

There are many guides on that journey, and Jesus is one of them. The mystic Jesus is not a theological construct; he is a spiritual force. He is a presence within us through which we can forge an intimate relationship with God, ourselves, and each other. He becomes a lived experience as we practice the principles that are the core of his message to the world. He is an intercession from a thought system beyond our own, a master healer of the human race.

Jesus is a bridge to another kind of thinking, better thought of as a living inner guide than as a stained-glass icon. He is a reminder of who and what we truly are.

He stands in the breach between the neurotic, weak, fearful, and judgmental you and the strong and powerful, forgiving and most glorious you. He can lead you from one to the other. His mind, joined with ours, can shine away the fear-laden sense of self that plagues us.

That is the revelation of the mystic Jesus. He will lead us through the darkness in our mind, to the light that God placed there and that cannot be erased. The mystic Jesus is not an idol. He is an evolutionary Elder Brother, not forcing himself on anyone but available to everyone. The subject of this book is who he is, and who we ourselves become when our thoughts align with his.

In 1992, I published a book called *A Return to Love*. In the chapter on forgiveness, I told my readers I totally understood that forgiveness could be hard. Why? *Because I had once been stood up for a date to the Olympics!*

I kid you not. In fact, not only was that the most extreme example I could come up with at the time for how hard it could be to forgive; I even remember others telling me that that was their favorite section of the book!

Oh my, what innocent times those were. I had not yet been deeply deceived in life, and I had not yet deeply deceived myself. I was giving myself kudos for forgiving someone who had merely stood me up for a date. I really had no idea—yet—how hard forgiveness could be.

Over time, life did to me what it does to everyone who lives long enough: it showed itself to me. And I've learned things I could never have learned had I not come to experience the harshness of the world. I've learned that behind my mistakes, and behind the mistakes of others, lies a corrective mechanism that some call grace.

As life got tougher, I began to realize that the cliché is true: you get bitter or you get better. If our habitual reaction to the lovelessness of the world is to toughen up, to wall ourselves off, then we will only experience more pain. For we actually create what we defend against, attracting to ourselves the very thing that we fear might happen. But we can choose a better way; we can replace our fears with love. Our safety lies not in defensiveness but in defenselessness. Perfect love is inviolable: we were not created to be vulnerable to the lovelessness in ourselves or others. It's not a mantle of attack but a mantle of forgiveness that will protect us from life's storms. Instead of trying to fight the world, we can realize the victory has already been won. We need not get more haggard and more weary as the years go by. Accepting the Atonement, seeing that only love is real, we come to understand that we might as well calm down. In any instant, we can accept what's true. And there we are released.

That is the mindset of enlightenment, the gift of the mystic Christ.

CHAPTER ONE

THE MYSTIC JESUS

A N EVENT OCCURRED two thousand years ago that changed the world, ultimately bringing to an end one era of human civilization and beginning another. The birth, teachings, crucifixion, and resurrection of one man, a Jew named Jesus, have overshadowed the march of history. In his name some of the greatest elements of civilization have emerged, and in his name some of the worst elements of civilization have emerged. He did not set out to found an institutional church, yet one arose that has claimed for millennia a monopoly on who he is.

Now, at a time of historic change, in order to pave a sustainable way forward, humanity needs to question everything that went before. Interpretations, philosophies, laws, concepts, assumptions, entire ways of being left over from the past are being reviewed, transformed, and renewed. And they must be. Humanity has reached a point in the road where the path of least resistance is a path toward global destruction. For we are stuck in ways of thinking and behaving that are rooted in war—war against ourselves, against each other, even against the earth it-self. These ways are not working. New ways are being born.

Since Jesus is fundamental to the worldview of billions of people on the planet, an inquiry into his identity and power plays a significant role in rethinking the world. The Jesus of traditional Christianity has a musty smell for many, while the mystic Jesus has a raw, transformational, and very modern power. The mystic path is the path of the psyche, and it is there that we are most shackled. We are shackled not by external chains but by spiritual ignorance, by a misunderstanding of who we are and why we are here. Jesus is a key to the unlocking of our internal imprisonment. Rather than lacking practical relevance, the mystic Jesus has a shattering effect on the illusions of meaninglessness that plague us. When looked at freed from the filter of centuries of predetermined interpretation, he does not fall away into insignificance but rather shines forth in an almost startling modern light. Jesus is as meaningful today as he was when he was born. In the words of St. Augustine, he is "ever ancient, ever new."

He was born two thousand years ago, but in very real ways we're only beginning to understand.

As the twenty-first century lurches ahead with full force, collective despair increases every day. From climate change to war to authoritarian uprisings, the era before us feels less like the promise of a bright future and more a demand that we pay for past mistakes. From environmental recklessness to military and economic imperialism to authoritarianism run amok, our past sins seem to be pressing down on us like IOUs that have all come suddenly due. Humanity is overwhelmed by its karmic debts, as though there are simply too many to pay back and retribution is now inevitable.

That's certainly one way to look at it, of course.

In truth, however, humanity is very much at choice as to what will happen next. Two starkly different futures stand before us: either the immeasurable suffering of human civilization in continuous decline, or the advent of a new world now struggling to be born. One is a world of global destruction, the other a world of global rebirth. Both are possibilities; in fact, both are already occurring.

Global decline results from humanity's accumulated greed and lovelessness, our continuing to do things the way we've been doing them. The possibility of rebirth emerges from our eternal yearning for the good and the true, and our willingness to radically change. The former violates the web of life, while the latter supports and aligns with it. From climate change to increasing nuclear and military threats, the world that's declining is declining fast, while the world that's emerging is emerging a bit too slowly. Right now we're in a frantic race for time.

This book is about the miracle of transformative change, a deliverance from our psychological propensity to self-annihilating thought and behavior. Such change is both deeply religious as well as deeply psychological. As *A Course in Miracles* says, psychotherapy and religion are at their peak the same thing. Both at their best are a healing of the mind, reconnecting the mind and heart in a way that rebalances the psyche and heals one's life. The mystic Jesus lies at the heart of that change. He is a generator of a celestial speedup, a process by which we leap beyond the confines of our current stage of evolution to become the people we need to be in order to save the world in time.

Have You Been Saved
by JEEZUS?!?

Decades ago, strolling through New York's Central Park one beautiful sunny day, my friend and I were approached by someone who in those days was called a "Jesus freak."

"Sister," the earnest stranger said to me beseechingly, "have you been *saaaved*?"

By that time I'd been a student of *A Course in Miracles* for a while.

"Well . . . ," I said slowly. "That actually depends on what you mean when you say that. If you mean, have I been saved by a higher power from the crazy, neurotic thoughts that otherwise perform like toxic forces to destroy my peace of mind, then I guess, yes, I would have to say that I have!" I nodded knowingly. "Psychologically, of course."

"But have you been saved by *JEEZUS*?!"

"That's a very interesting question you're asking," I said. "Because if you think of Jesus as in fact a personification of Love, a force of consciousness that is the ultimate Reality within me and all human beings, then I guess, yes, I have been saved by Jesus.

I mean, it totally changed my life! But if you're talking about a doctrinal, dogmatic principle of institutionalized religion then I would have to say no, not really, because..."

Our new friend looked thoroughly flummoxed, almost as if he'd seen a ghost. I remember my boyfriend taking me firmly by the arm and saying, "Marianne, let's just keep walking."

The young man we encountered that day was talking about something very different than I was. He had found his understanding of Jesus in an institutionalized setting, his Jesus narrowly defined by a specific dogmatic interpretation.

I found mine in *A Course in Miracles*.

And at Christie's...

In 2017, I was living in New York and received a phone call from my friend Maria. She told me she had a friend who worked at Christie's auction house, which had Leonardo da Vinci's *Salvator Mundi* on display. Would I want to see it?

I had read about the picture that morning, how a painting of Christ considered by scholars to be a Leonardo original had just been purchased by a mystery buyer. The painting was on display at Christie's but was going to be removed that afternoon.

I was curious to see it, and I was grateful to Maria for calling. She and I agreed to meet at the auction house, where we were led by her friend to the short line still left at the end of the viewing period. We were just chatting casually as though this was any other museum or gallery visit–until I stood before the painting, that is.

Within a moment, I was stunned.

Here was a painting of Jesus, dressed in blue Renaissance robes, making the sign of the cross with his right hand and in his left holding a clear crystal orb signaling the celestial spheres of heaven. I gazed at the painting, and it was beautiful, of course. But as I continued to gaze at it something mysterious began to happen; the painting turned into something more.

I have never had an experience quite like it. I'd seen Leonardo's *Mona Lisa* and Michelangelo's *Pietà* and *David*, plus many other great pieces of art. I have visited some of the greatest museums in the world. But I had never seen anything like what I saw that day. *I was somehow delivered beyond the painting.* Salvator Mundi became some kind of portal to what lay behind it, to what Jesus is on some level that had never before been revealed to me. I saw something I didn't even know existed.

It sounds kind of silly, but it was *words* that I experienced. It was as though I was transported inside two words, as though they were not just words but somehow realms of experience. The words themselves were simple enough: they were "tenderness" and "power."

I saw that Jesus is both those things in infinite degree. He is a gentleness more tender than the kisses of a billion babies, and at the same time a power so powerful it creates and manages universes. How such things exist I do not know, but I saw them when I looked at *Salvator Mundi*.

I was left alone to stare at the painting, the last person to see it before movers came to take it away. Maria and I left Christie's, but my thoughts were still with the painting and my experience as I looked at it. I was curious who the mystery buyer might be, and I kept scouring the internet for information. *Who*, I kept thinking, *was the human being who would get to have this treasure in their possession?*

A couple of hours later the buyer's identity was announced, and I was shocked. For the purchaser was none other than Mohammed bin Salman, the dictatorial Saudi Arabian prince who would soon be involved in the alleged murder of Jamal Khashoggi. MBS had bought the painting for $450 million as the centerpiece of the new Louvre Abu Dhabi.

It all just felt so wrong. How could MBS, of all people, be the purchaser? How could a brutal dictator be able to purchase such a priceless jewel? Then after a minute or two, my thinking changed. What could possibly be a more powerful thing? This wasn't wrong; it couldn't be more right. Jesus is *Salvator Mundi*, after all. Where else, and with whom else, would the savior of the world possibly wish to be?

In His Name

With all the churches that have been built in the name of Jesus, and all the wars that have been fought in his name, why is there so little love in his name? With roughly a third of humanity professing devotion to Jesus of Nazareth, why is the world such a desperately sorrowful and violent place for so many of the world's inhabitants?

The problem is not with Jesus; the problem is with us. People praise him and espouse him and build edifices to honor him. Yet the world remains in spiritual darkness. While billions say they believe in Jesus, belief means nothing in the absence of lived experience. It is a deeper manifestation of his love for which the world yearns now.

"It is time to inject a new dimension of love into the veins of human civilization," said the Reverend Dr. Martin Luther King Jr. That dimension of love is a mystic and universal love, emerging anew from the human heart and illuminating the human brain. Calling on Jesus is one way to invoke that love.

In order to understand the emergence of this mystic Jesus, it helps to go back in time. Then we can understand more clearly how his light became so obscured to begin with.

Following the death of Jesus, two major arteries of thought developed around his life and teachings. One would become the ecclesiastical Christian church. This tradition emphasizes doctrine and dogma, plus the role of the church in overseeing and guiding our relationship to God. This artery represents an external, or exoteric, orientation, with the church a material gateway—and gatekeeper—to the understanding of our spiritual reality.

A second artery, often rejected by traditional Christian churches, has nevertheless exerted a continuous pull on the human heart. Mystics such as Teresa of Ávila, Julian of Norwich, Meister Eckhart, Teilhard de Chardin, the Celtic saints, and the Gnostic Gospels contained in the Nag Hammadi manuscripts have elucidated teachings of Christ based not on the externalized doctrines of an organized church but on an inner relationship with the divine. Mystic teachings represent an internal, or esoteric, orientation: a spiritual path to a more enlightened understanding of the deeper meaning of our lives. Mystics have been appreciated by many throughout history, yet they've often been driven underground, both literally and figuratively. At times they've been marginalized and even violently rejected when refusing to bow to the church's drive for power and control.

A contest between the two orientations has raged for centuries—sometimes violently, sometimes subtly—and in a way still does. The mystic Jesus emerging today arises from our collective consciousness, responding to a modern yearning for a healing of our hearts and minds not found in religious doctrine alone. *A Course in Miracles* is part of the ancient mystic legacy, particularly relevant for an age when the nature of the psyche, and of the larger universe, are core to our quest for meaning.

The mystic Jesus is an aspect of consciousness, alive in each of us, not as an abstraction but as a lived experience. The dark night into which the baby Jesus was born in Bethlehem is very much the dark sky of our modern world, and the star that heralds his birth is signaling the birth of something new within us.

In our arrogance we think so much has changed in the past two thousand years, but in some fundamental ways it has not. Humanity is still stumbling about in darkness. With our young killing each other and killing themselves at such an alarming rate, the earth itself buckling under the weight of our misuse, and weapons we've created perched to incinerate us all in the space of an hour, we cannot truthfully tell ourselves that things are going well.

The savagery and barbarism of times past are reflected in horrifying ways among us now, our minds gripped in a vise from which we seemingly cannot escape. For all the genius that has graced the world throughout human history, intellectual knowledge and the expertise of our greatest minds have not saved us. Nor will they. The power of the brain is extraordinary, but by itself it will not save us from ourselves. The heart alone is our salvation.

The mystic Jesus is a deeper alignment of heart and mind, redirecting human intelligence and reminding us who we are. He was a historic figure, of course, but he is ahistorical as well. He was present as a man on the earth two thousand years ago, and he is present as a spirit within our psyches even now. He is a name for the unalterable love that all of us share, out of which we were created and through which all of us are one.

What Is the Christ?

Imagine a time in life when you were happiest. Wasn't it a time when any feeling of separation from the world, or separation from another human being, had vanished? Whether hiking in the wilderness or sailing on the open sea, whether witnessing the birth of a baby or holding a lover in your arms, wasn't there a moment when you felt you had a glimpse of what life was meant to be?

Everyone alive has a haunting memory of a primordial oneness, like an ancient melody we can't quite get out of our heads. "A memory of home keeps haunting you, as if there were a place that called you to return, although you do not recognize the voice, nor what it is the voice reminds you of"* (WB-339). It is a song that beckons us, the sound of which we cannot escape. And we seek through whatever means possible to reclaim it.

Drugs, alcohol, sex, shopping, whatever activity provides even a momentary escape from the dullness of our ordinary human existence, we're all over it. We know on some level that the world as we find it here is not the world that we wish to inhabit. For this world is not our spiritual home; its roots are not deep enough to sustain us. We come from somewhere beyond this world, from an oceanic realm of bliss that is the Mind of God. In that primordial bliss we were created, and to that primordial bliss we long to return. Our disconnection from that state of being has left us in chronic though subconscious hysteria and grief. We long unceasingly for the memory of who we are.

God is an infinite ocean of Love, not figuratively but literally, of which we are part and from which we cannot be separated. We are ideas in His Mind, and "ideas leave not their source"* (WB-242). We have the power to forget what's true, but we don't have the power to establish what's true. We are like children of the wealthiest, most powerful father who have forgotten our identity and the inheritance that comes with it. We wander endlessly in search of something that cannot be found but only realized.

The world as we know it perpetuates our forgetfulness, constantly disrupting our relationship to God by disrupting our relationship to each other. Not remembering Him, we do not remember ourselves, and not remembering ourselves, we do not remember one another. The world teaches us we are separate from Him and from That on which our very existence depends. The world teaches us that we are who we are not and that we are not who we are. It teaches us that the world is meaningless, when in fact we are its meaning. Our souls are wounded, and in our woundedness we suffer.

Healing, therefore, lies in remembering who we are.

We are more than just bodies who die; we are spirits who live forever. We are not just an accumulation of worldly experiences, some good and some bad; we are an unalterable innocence that lies forever at the heart of who we are. And through the presence of God within us, with our love we are infinitely powerful.

In making that shift from a crude and delusional to a transcendent sense of self, we change everything. Enlightenment is a shift in self-perception from body-identification to spirit-identification, paving the way out of spiritual darkness into spiritual light. On the level of the body, we are weighed down by the world; on the level of spirit, we are lifted above it. On the level of the body, we are separate; on the level of spirit, we are one.

Imagine a wheel with an infinite number of spokes. Now imagine that every person in the world is a spoke. Normally, we'd identify spokes by their position on the wheel, where they are separate from all the other spokes.

Yet our ultimate identity is not our position on the rim. Our spiritual reality is where the spokes begin, at the hub of the wheel. There we are one with all the other spokes, at a mystical source point that is both our beginning and our end. One name for that source point, that mystical oneness, is the Christ. The Christ is a name for our ultimate Reality, the bedrock spiritual foundation of who we really are.

If you go deep enough into your mind and deep enough into mine, we share mental images that Carl Jung called universal archetypes in our collective unconscious. The idea of the Christ mind takes things one step further. At the deepest level, we don't just share images; we actually share one mind. That is the esoteric meaning of the line "There is only one begotten Son." In the realm of bodies, there are billions of us on the planet. On the level of spirit, only one of us is here.

To traditional Christians, Jesus the man was the one begotten Son. To the mystic, the Sonship is more than one man. It is the joining of all of us. It is God's creation, through which we are united eternally with God and with each other, never to be separate except within an illusion of the mind. The evidence of the physical senses reveals a world of separation; the evidence of the heart reveals we are one. And the illusion of our separation does not just deceive; it causes us great pain. We find real comfort only in the truth of the heart.

When I first began studying the *Course*, I was in my midtwenties. For many people, that is a most difficult decade. The innocence of childhood is replaced by what is often a brutal awakening to the realities of the modern world, causing a distress to the psyche that can be quite extreme. This anxiety is not always a dysfunctional response to the insanity of our time, but rather a functional one. It is a call to spiritually awaken. Just as physical pain is a signal to attend to a physical wound, psychic pain can be a signal to attend to a spiritual one. All of us at one point or another receive an urgent call from the depth of our souls to remember who we are and why we're here. We are love, and we are here to love. We are mind, and on the level of mind we are one. Everything else is false information.

The world we live in has atomized our existence, turning everything into a commodity and every person into a consumer. It is dominated by soulless forces that seek to demystify the ultimate mystery of our existence. It has trapped our minds in mental cages, filters through which we are trained to perceive ourselves and others in misguided ways. Within those filters there is no higher meaning. There is no transcendence. There is no rest for the soul.

The journey of enlightenment is not a learning but an unlearning—unlearning those attitudinal strictures that have boxed us in and stolen our joy. We come to see that we are not just material beings, trapped in the confines of our mortal existence. As creations of God, we are so much more. "Christ" is a word for that "so much more": our higher Self, our spiritual reality, our life beyond the limitations of the body.

To think we are nothing but the physical self is simply an illusion. Just as a plane taking off appears from the ground to get smaller as it flies into the sky, just as the earth feels still although it's moving at thousands of miles per hour, and just as matter is made up of tiny particles we can't see with the naked eye, the reality of the spiritual self, while unseen by the physical eye, is our ultimate reality nonetheless. Christ is the inner self that lies seemingly trapped beneath the illusions of the world. To remember it is a form of "salvation" because it saves us from an illusion of who we are.

The Light in which we were created and through which we are inseparable from God and from each other is real whether we believe it or not, just as the earth is round though many believed it was flat. We're like people in a very bright room putting our fingers in front of our eyes and complaining that it's dark in here. The ego is merely the false belief that we are separate. It is a self-perpetuating illusion chaining us to repeated misperceptions of ourselves and those around us; enlightenment is the process by which we burst free of those chains and by so doing help free others.

Enlightenment begins as an abstract concept, then takes a journey without distance from the head to the heart. Of course, it seems "real" to us that someone was unkind or mean to us, that we were rejected or failed to achieve something we desperately wanted, or that an important relationship failed. Of course, it seems "real" to us that innocent people are murdered, unjust wars occur, and people starve to death. Those things are real in our mortal experience, and they should not be ignored. But such dramas are happening within a world that is itself a veil in front of a truer truth—a world of three-dimensional reality that, while real in one sense, is not our ultimate Reality. They are the manifestations of humanity having forgotten who we are, and they will change accordingly when we wake up and remember.

As we move further into a new millennium, who among us does not feel a sense that the world as we know it is fundamentally askew, as evidenced not just in our individual lives but in the very way that we are living on the planet? Who doesn't recognize that constant examples of violence and destruction are symptoms of a deeper disquiet? Who isn't looking in some way for a higher purpose, a deeper sense of meaning, and a transformed sense of self?

Such questioning is when the spiritual quest begins. And once it begins, the path opens before us. Asking deep in our hearts for a way past the insanity of the world, we are led—often circuitously, always mysteriously—to something that opens the inner door.

The mystic Jesus is one name on that door. He is someone whose mind was purified of any thoughts of separation, or illusion, and who has been authorized by God to help the rest of us achieve that state should we so ask. In no moment does he succumb to the lure of ego, and with his help we can learn not to succumb to it either. The door having been opened within him, he has the power to help open it within us. He is not the only path to God, but if he is yours then you come to realize it. He is an Internal Teacher, an evolutionary guide back to the primordial oneness to which our souls so long to return. He is called Jesus the Christ because he lived in the world of illusion yet remembered a higher truth. He perceived this world yet saw beyond it. He lived outwardly on the material plane yet inwardly on the spiritual. In him the two became as one.

Since all minds are joined, the spiritual achievement of anyone then becomes available to all. In remembering the mystic Jesus, we remember who we are and who others are in relation to us. In calling on him we invoke our true selves, the memory of which saves us from the misguided thinking that otherwise torments us.

All false beliefs emerge from the misperception that we are separate. A thought that we are separate is like a shadow before the sun, keeping us in emotional darkness. We think we are worse than others, or we think we are better than others; we think they are judging us, or we are judging them; we attack and defend in a chronic, self-perpetuating loop. We live in a constant hell of believing we are separate from those from whom we cannot be separate. We long for love, we long for the feeling of that primordial oneness, yet we constantly think and behave in ways that make the separation seem real.

Guilt is the ego's most powerful tool, and the pain it causes us is its peak experience. Jesus is like a rope that will lift us from a bottomless well of anxiety, an escape from the hell of our own self-hatred. In teaching us to forgive each other, he shows us how to love ourselves.

Do unto others what you would have others do unto you, because what you do to them you actually *are* doing to yourself. The Golden Rule is golden for that reason: what I think about you or do to you, I *am* thinking about or doing to myself.

In a realm beyond what our physical senses perceive, there is no place where you stop and I start. In judging you I am judging myself; in attacking you I am attacking myself. Whatever I give to you I am giving to myself. As we realize this higher Truth, notions of separate identities and conflicting needs are dissolved into the nothingness from whence they came. As we realize we are spiritually one, we become "generous out of self-interest"* (MT-14). Our perceptions are recalibrated, giving us a far different sense of our responsibility to others.

So simple. Yet so much easier said than done.

The illusions of the world are strong, none more so than the perception of someone's guilt. Knowing that beyond a person's mistake lies the innocence of their soul is easy enough to accept in theory, but boy, it's very hard at times to get there. Sometimes taking the leap from knowing a person is spiritually innocent to perceiving them that way is more than we can achieve by ourselves.

Jesus is someone with the authority, should we request it, to enter our minds and share with us his ability to love unconditionally. Sometimes it's easy enough to just lighten up, to let something go. But sometimes it's not so easy at all. Someone truly betrayed us, or triggered the deepest of childhood wounds. It feels at such times that it would take a miracle for us to forgive. The mystic Jesus *is* that miracle. "Your mind and mine can unite in shining your ego away, releasing the strength of God into everything you think and do"* (T-64).

He cannot enter our thought system uninvited, for that would be a violation of our free will. But if we take a moment, even a moment, and call to him, he will "respond fully to your slightest invitation"* (T-90). He is authorized by God to help us in any moment we're willing to see beyond the separation. Our good intentions are not enough, but our willingness is everything. When we're sincerely willing to see beyond the veil of illusion—the thoughts of guilt we are all so good at—to the innocent truth of who all of us are, we experience a shift in perception. That shift is a miracle, changing us on the level of thought and ultimately changing our lives.

Let's say you're having an argument with someone you love. They're attacking and you're defending yourself, or you're attacking and they're defending. Usually in such cases, of course you're sure you're right! The wheel of suffering goes round and round, nailing you to the cross of your own misery and destroying the fabric of your relationship. People today will give you an endless array of terms for what's going on between you, from "trauma," to "victimization," to "post-traumatic stress disorder," to "narcissism." All of which might be true, and might need to be looked at. But none of those terms, or their analysis, will deliver you from the hell of your own suffering until you make your way to forgiveness. For in holding on to someone else's guilt, we are holding on to our own. Our willingness to see through to another person's innocence—extending our perception beyond the level of their mistake to knowledge of who they truly are—is the forgiveness that sets us free.

Just stop for a moment. Be willing to interrupt the cycle of what might be by now a somewhat vicious back-and-forth. Take a deep breath and remember that "beyond this world there is a world I want"* (WB-235)—a Reality that lies beyond this world. Silently bless the other person; perhaps inwardly atone for your own participation in the ridiculousness of how you have both behaved. If you ask Jesus to help you, he will. Tell him you're willing to see this person the way he does—they in their innocence, and you in yours. Just take that one instant, send love, pray for a miracle, and then notice what begins to happen. Prayer is the medium of miracles* (T-3), and it never goes unheard.

Dear God,
Please show me how to see this differently.
Show me how to see beyond the illusions of the world.
I am willing to see this person's innocence,
and I am willing to see mine.
Dear God, I am so triggered.
I cannot see past my feelings of insult or injury.
But I am willing to.
May the mind of Jesus overshadow
mine, and lift me as he is lifted,
that I might be set free.
Amen

As you do this, subtle shifts will begin to occur. Something will be said, other things will not be said. Things will change. All minds are joined, and on a subconscious level the other person experienced your blessing. As you released your judgment, you released yourself. You didn't need more analysis here. You needed a miracle. And you received one.

The world as we know it is dominated by the ego's thought system and it can be overwhelmingly strong. Its lure is like a heat-seeking missile, constantly on alert to the tiniest evidence of another person's guilt. Why? Because as long as I think you're guilty–of anything, even the slightest thing–then I will not see you are one with me. I will then feel pain that in my spiritual ignorance I think is due to something that you did. In fact my pain is due to my denying your innocence, for in denying your perfection I am denying my own.

Free will allows us to do this all day every day, and most of us to some extent do. We attack, we judge, we defend, we withhold–constantly deflecting the love that is our natural inheritance. There is, however, another way. "Eventually everyone begins to recognize, however dimly, that there must be a better way. As this recognition becomes more firmly established, it becomes a turning point"* (T-22). The mystic Jesus is exactly that. Think of him as a better way. The most powerful thing we can do when we're in mental torment about anything is to say to ourselves the following: "I am determined to see this differently"* (WB-32). Our greatest power to change the world lies in our power to think about it differently.

The mystic Jesus is a bridge of perception between who we are when we are lost in ego, and who we are when we are at home in God. He is like someone who helps us cross the river when we're too tired to go on. He's not above us, but he is ahead of us in time, like a gentle guide reaching out to a stumbling child and lifting us above the rocks.

Jesus closes the gap between who we truly are and who we too often think we are. When we think and behave in ways that are not true to our real selves—tied to fear-based reactions based on wounds from the past—he enters into the breach between our eternal reality and the false, fractal self that would replace it. He cannot enter without an invitation, for free will reigns supreme. But we cannot call on him in vain.

Having fully ascended into the ethers of pure love, Jesus has gained the authority to override the ego's dictates. Having achieved full actualization within himself, he has the power to intercede on our behalf when fear has hacked our internal operating system and hides the truth of who we are.

When Michelangelo was asked how he created a statue, he said that when he went to the quarry to look at pieces of marble, he imagined that God had already created the statue of *David* or *Moses*, or the *Pietà* and so forth. Michelangelo saw his job as removing the excess marble that surrounded the perfect statue already existing within it.

We're both the statue within the marble as well as the sculptor who makes it visible. Hiding inside the marble is the truth of who we are. God has already created the perfect you and me, for we are thoughts within His Mind. Our mission is to rid ourselves of the accumulated marble that has been added since we got here, all the layers of dysfunction and fear resulting from our exposure to the pain of the world.

We are then left "naked and unashamed," stripped of the layers of fear and falsehood now surrounding our true self. Like plaque that can build up in the body and decrease blood flow to the heart, a mental plaque builds up within our minds. Our spiritual purpose is to unlearn the fear built up in our psyches, to remember the innocence and love that is the truth of who we are.

As our true self is the statue within the marble, Jesus is a sculptor who can work with us to make it visible. If you were able to drop your fear, your anger, your neuroses, your anxiety, your character defects, your judgments, your addictions, your armor, your defensiveness, your attack thoughts, and your sense of victimization, there would be one thing left: the real you. And that is the Christ within.

Jesus is one who became that true self. He is the actualized potential of what a human being can be. He is both a template and a guide to the self we wish to be in the world. Jesus is an example, a teacher, and a gift. He is a mystic power that can take us home.

The Only Story Ever Told

The life of Jesus is like a hologram that reveals to us the mysteries of the universe. The more we penetrate the mysteries of his life, the more deeply we understand our own. The story of the spirit is the story of the psyche, not only his but also ours. His birth, life, crucifixion, and resurrection are not just the stuff of exoteric religion; they are codes and clues and harbingers of a different kind of existence. They are not just metaphors; they are principles that activate a reality that lies beyond this world.

Beyond this world there is a world we want, a world revealed not by the outer eye but by an inner eye. That world is an eternal reality unseen because it is eclipsed, hidden as with a veil by an egoic, fear-based worldview.

The world beyond that veil is a world of endless love, the one ultimate reality, the Mind of God. It isn't evident because it's hidden from our view, yet we are the ones who are hiding it. We hide it with the kinds of thoughts we think. We have denied ourselves vision of that world by denying it is there.

The light we seek is not something to be found but something to be chosen, not something we can get but only something we can give. It's not some other place but rather another realm of perception. It is the same life we are living now, transformed by love.

The opening of the inner eye is not symbolic; it's what happens when the veil is removed and we can see. My inner eye was opened, if only for a moment, when I looked at *Salvator Mundi*. I glimpsed another world in all its tenderness and power. It was a world invoked by forgiveness, in which our willingness to bless each other is far stronger than our temptation to blame, and the power of an infinite love casts out the power of fear.

The mystic Jesus casts out fear, thus breaking the chain of evil and returning us to our right minds. In the presence of his love, the fear dissolves. And the spirit is reborn.

Jesus was a man, yes, but he is also a spirit as alive today as he was two thousand years ago. The birth of Jesus as a physical being was the birth of the historical Christ; the advent of divine love into our thinking is the birth of Christ into the world today. He does not appear now as a man but as a state of consciousness, which does not make him any less real. The very concept of reality is transforming as we move further into the twenty-first century, humanity evolving beyond the limited framework of primacy given to external factors at the expense of internal forces. Once we recognize that the world of matter is simply a world of effects, the causes of which lie in consciousness, we begin to pay much more attention to the goings-on of the inner life.

We will not stop war or environmental degradation or world hunger or rampant addiction or any of the stresses that plague us today until we address the inner dynamics—the perversions of heart—that give rise to them. The problem of world hunger, for instance, is not hunger itself; the problem is that the people of the world find it tolerable that a child should starve. There is no dearth of food. There is only a dearth of willingness to put love for our fellow human beings before our acquiescence to a system that in essence doesn't care if children starve. Global poverty is a symptom, not a cause. Its cause is our collective disconnection from adherence to the principles of a moral cosmos. That Jesus works with us on the level of cause, on the plane of consciousness, does not make him less relevant but even more relevant to the practical concerns of humanity today.

The Second Coming is synonymous with the evolution of humanity into our self-actualized state. The Second Coming isn't the reappearance of someone who left and will return; it's a remembrance of what has never left but has been obscured. The mystic Jesus is the Alpha and Omega that always was and always will be. His reappearance in the world means our remembrance of who we are.

How many times have people said to me, "I don't know who I am," or "I can't find a place for myself in this world," or "I don't think I even belong here." The world blinds us to who we are and why we're here. The world as we know it is not home to the true self, and we cannot find ourselves within its walls. Even at its best it is a rickety, shoddy house compared to the light-filled mansion that exists within.

Yet the point is not to ignore the world or to reject it. We are here to transform it. Our purpose is to become the light that casts out the darkness, to be harbingers of a different world by becoming different people. The more we understand the deeper meaning of events, the more powerful we are at transforming them.

The deeper meaning of any situation is a universal longing for love. All of us long for it; all of us are looking for it. The miracle occurs when we realize we ourselves are here to provide it.

We can see God's love only when we are willing to express it.

We cannot find what we are looking for without realizing *who* we are. I think of all the years I was struggling so hard to "find God," not realizing that I would see His love manifest in my own life only when I sought to make it manifest in the lives of others. Any wall we build to keep out others will keep God out of our conscious awareness. The only way to find His love is by giving it away.

The mystical birth of Jesus is the opening of the heart. Just as Mary gave birth to the historical Jesus, the mystic Jesus enters the world through us. He is born any moment that we are willing to give birth to him. He is born again in any moment of unconditional love. This isn't simply an abstract idea; it's a practical moment we either do or do not choose.

In every moment we are making a choice, whether we make it consciously or we make it unconsciously. We can either open our heart or close it, and our lives unfold accordingly. In every instant we are generating a thought, and every thought will have an effect.

How often we choose to blame instead of bless, judge instead of accept, take instead of give. And why? Because we were trained to think that way. The ego constantly tempts us to separate ourselves off from the rest of the universe. But the mystic Jesus has the power to override the ego's dictates, to save us from our chronic temptation to withhold our love. Choosing to align with him, we cocreate with God a different kind of world.

Our power to work miracles lies in our choice to think differently. Choosing forgiveness, choosing to extend our perceptions beyond the level of someone's guilt, choosing to see ourselves as present in any situation to be the presence of love, we align our minds with the Mind of God and rise above the ego. The thinking of the world is no longer like quicksand that sucks us into it. The vibrations of higher consciousness—that is, thoughts of love—

make us invulnerable to the chaos that dominates the world. In fact, they make us its transformers.

And that is the miracle. A miracle begins as a shift in our thinking, a change on the causal level of things that then transforms the realm of effects. Even the tiniest candle casts out darkness. "All expressions of love are maximal"* (T-3), like a tincture of God's power that makes all the difference. Even the tiniest thought of forgiveness, of mercy, of love, can change the trajectory of our lives.

I learned at a seminar years ago a technique that I've passed on to many others. We were told to look at people and silently say to them, "The love in me salutes the love in you." How often I've been in situations where I've done that and seen extraordinary changes. For all minds are joined. The vast majority of data we receive is registered subconsciously. We can feel it when we are being judged, and we can feel it when we are being loved. Our greatest power to effect change begins with our power to think differently. There is no greater preparation for a meeting than to blast the room with love before we get there. It changes the meeting because it changes *you*. How you show up in life—not only what you do, but who you are—determines in large part the reactions of those around you.

Love is the organizing principle of the universe. Just as the body organically organizes itself, so does the universe when we allow it to. And just as the body has a tremendous capacity to heal itself when something has gone wrong, so does the rest of life.

Miracles are the natural unfoldment of the universe, an expression of the Mind of God as every loving thought is followed by another loving thought. "Miracles are natural. When they do not occur something has gone wrong"* (T-3). What has "gone wrong" is a wrong-minded thought—that is, a loveless one. But God's universe is like a GPS. As soon as we take a wrong turn, the GPS simply recalculates our path. That recalculation, that return to right-minded thinking when the heart has been closed, is called the Atonement. The world is moving in a dangerous direction because our collective thought patterns are infused with irreverence. This is the century to turn things around. This will be a century of miracles, if we so choose.

As someone whose mind has been purified of all ego thought, Jesus has become one with the Atonement. In calling on him we are reaching for divine correction: the thought, the feeling, the situation that will free us from the ego's grip. He is a portal to a different world because he is a portal to a different kind of thought.

He cannot do for us, however, what he cannot do through us. Without our willingness, the miracle cannot occur. When we are willing to forgive, be merciful, be gentle, be kind, then we are allowing our lives to be channels for his appearance. And when he appears the world is made new. Thinking of ourselves as vessels through which God is trying to express Himself, the birth of Christ begins to make sense on a psychological and emotional level. The light Jesus brings to the world is the light he brings to *your* world. When we are more compassionate, more forgiving, then our lives begin to change.

So often we're busy searching for an answer to a problem, unaware that the answer begins with us—with the way we're speaking to others, thinking of others, or behaving toward others. The solution to whatever problem confronts us is always available within the ethers of an unlimited universe, simply blocked when our hearts are closed. Love in our hearts—and most important, expressed in our behavior—attracts help, respect, and willingness to help us when we need it. When our hearts are closed, we deflect the miracles we desperately need and long for.

I remember years ago when I would sit in a therapist's office complaining about how hard it was for me to attract support in my office. So much time and money I spent trying to analyze what had happened in my childhood to create the pattern I constantly reenacted. If only even one therapist had thought to ask me, "Can we look at how you behave toward those who are trying to support you? Do you realize that in your pain you close your heart to others? You are responsible for your effects in life. Your childhood is not an excuse; no matter where you got the problem, it's yours now, and you are responsible for it. No matter what happened in your past, the miracle lies in who you choose to be now." It wasn't analysis of the problem that freed me, it was a prayer for a miracle: "Dear God, where I am harsh, please make me gentle."

How profound that love truly is the Answer. Salvation itself isn't complicated, and perhaps that's the reason we so often ignore it. We think it can't be that easy, that the answers to our problems must surely be more complicated than simply choosing love. Yet "complexity is of the ego"* (T-310). The truth is very simple, really. If a child is hungry, you feed them. Voilà.

Choosing love is not what's difficult; what's difficult is getting over our resistance to choosing love. The ego comes up with very complicated reasons why love is rarely the right answer, using the power of our own minds to obscure the obvious. The ego makes strength appear as weakness and weakness appear as strength.

The ego's thought system is like a consciousness hack, and the mystic Jesus unhacks it. He transforms the world by transforming us. He transforms our attitudes, our nervous systems, and our relationship to others. It is not hyperbole to say that he gives us new life.

From the immaculate conception to the annunciation, from his birth to his family's flight into Egypt, from his teaching in the temple to his baptism, from his temptation to his transfiguration, from Gethsemane to the crucifixion, from his resurrection to his ascension, the life of Jesus has meaning on both outer and inner planes. Yes, those are stories, but they are also states of awareness. All stages of his life have mystical equivalents. The birth of every child is the birth of God's love, or the birth of love into the world. The thinking of the world then inevitably violates all of us, leading to pain and despair; that is the meaning of the crucifixion. When we choose to respond with forgiveness, love prevails; that is the meaning of the resurrection. The lesson of the resurrection is that love corrects all things.

That's not just the story of our lives; in some ways it's the story of almost every situation. Everyone's life is different, with unique circumstances and experiences. Yet on another level there is only one story. Every single moment, we're living out the same one.

The dynamic of the life of Jesus—his birth, his crucifixion, and his resurrection—is a template for a deeper understanding of the human experience. As we recognize the workings of those dynamics, we're empowered to claim the miracle of resurrection in our own lives. In him it is already done. The power of the ego has been overcome in one; therefore his overcoming is available to all. The point is not to share the crucifixion of Jesus, but to share in his resurrection.

Understanding the mystical journey makes it easier, quicker, more miraculous.

Mary's Love

Just as the figures in a dream are various aspects of who we are, so are the figures in scripture. The mystical Mary represents the human heart, the receptive feminine aspect of the psyche.

Humanity is pregnant with a new phase of its history, and for most of us it's a difficult pregnancy. Every life is a microcosm of the evolutionary changes occurring in the world. We're experiencing rebirth as individuals as well as the rebirth of human civilization. We're either headed for a death spiral, or else we are preparing for something new. That something new will not emerge just from science or politics; it will emerge from within us.

The esoteric dimensions of Mary's story hold deep meaning for the modern seeker. She was a maiden blessed by God, awakened in the middle of the night by the angel Gabriel and told to go up onto the roof. There, she was told by the angel she would give birth to the Son of God.

Mary's was said to be a virgin birth, of course, yet what we read as the word "virgin" today meant simply "maiden" in the original Greek. The idea that Mary was impregnated by God rather than by man has mystical significance whether she was physically a virgin or not. There is something that happens in our hearts when we feel a stirring, a sense we can't quite put our finger on, that something new is about to happen. It does not come from anything or anyone outside us. It's unfolding from deep within.

Mary is the feminine yin to God's masculine yang. God impregnates the human heart. What is born from that divine conception is the Christ, a new sense of self that we carry into the world. This newborn self is fathered by God and mothered by our humanness, the truth of who we are, both human and divine.

It's not just Mary who was awakened from her sleep; all humanity has been in a state of spiritual slumber. "Yet the Bible says that a deep sleep fell upon Adam, and nowhere is there reference to his waking up"* (T-18). Who among us isn't feeling the call to awaken?

Our personal awakening is a gradual process, not necessarily a eureka moment heralding a dramatic change. There might not have been a particular moment or event, or anything that even seemed very significant at the time. It might have been a prayer or meditation or mindfulness practice. It might have been a relationship or a book or a teacher or a spiritual journey. It could have been any form of life-changing experience, good or bad, that cracked open the heart and led to greater wisdom. It might have been an almost eerie experience of simply knowing something, though we couldn't explain why. No matter what form our initial awakening took, we remember it as something that formed a crack in our resistance and signaled the arrival of something new. It was that something that awakened us from our sleep and led us to the "roof" of our higher mind.

Mary was to tell no one, and neither are we. The birth of new life is a mysterious process, whether it's the birth of a child or the birth of a better self.

The period of gestation requires nourishment and care. We

have an instinctive understanding that certain ideas should stay within us, protected from outside exposure until they're ready to be brought forth. The spiritual life is difficult to cultivate amid the clanging clamor of the modern world. Not just within Mary, but also within us, the newborn Christ needs protection. It isn't safe in this society to talk about our spiritual lives in just any old setting. Conscious friendships, therapists, and spiritual or religious counselors offer protected spaces. Outside those, it can be emotionally treacherous to share our deepest feelings about the inner life.

And what is being born from deep within us is the power that will save the world. Mary represents a facet of consciousness often referred to as the "divine feminine," a long-suppressed dimension of both self and society that is desperately needed now. "This is what is meant by 'the meek shall inherit the earth.' They will literally take it over because of their strength"* (T-20). Mary's powers of kindness, gentleness, tenderness, nurturing, bravery, understanding, and mystery—and most of all, her endurance amid the deepest grief—are all aspects of self that will help us build a more sustainable world.

Like Mary, we too feel the stirring of new life within us. Like her, we keep these things within us and we ponder them in our hearts. The whisper of angels is a deeply personal thing. Sometimes it's insight, the intuitional hits we get in the middle of the night. Some mysterious force is encouraging us to be better, to do better, than we have ever been or done before. We have a feeling that changes are coming and that we have some work to do.

The future of the world depends on our doing it. It will take more than physical acts of procreation to perpetuate the life of humanity now; it will take an evolution of human consciousness, a collective wisdom that does not yet exist on a massive scale. And just as physical life gestates within the body, wisdom gestates within the mind. We must be and do differently now in order for the species to survive.

The ego, of course, will have none of that. Herod—the ego writ large—is always on the lookout. The ego jealously guards its power lest love take primacy over its worldly interests. It seeks to invalidate and destroy all expressions of love. Herod wasn't having any of it with that powerful baby who was born to be King of the Jews. He would rather kill all the babies than allow that one to live. Mary was obviously very vulnerable then, as all of us feel when new life—whether physical or spiritual—grows within us.

Where does our protection lie?

It lies in Joseph, the "divine masculine," the aspect of the psyche that manages the material world. It makes sure we're safe as we go through our transformational process. Joseph received all the instruction he needed. He was directed to take Mary to Egypt to protect her, just as we learn appropriate self-care and the gifts of solitude. The land of Egypt means the sacred self; we retreat to that place within us while the old order falls away, incubating our powers until the hour when the culture is ready to receive it.

Herod's edict to "kill all Jewish babies" means the ego's desire to nip in the bud any emerging hope. Herod's sons represent newer generations of egoic figures, always working to suppress the voices of those who might emerge as a challenge to the old order. The voice of the mystic finds no welcome in Herod's land, but God is with you. You will be delivered to the manger, a very humble place within your heart. And there you will give birth.

Absolutely that birth is the salvation of the world. You, like Mary, give birth to the Christ—anytime you enter the present free of the past and with nothing in your heart but love. Worldly kings will get off their "high horses" when they realize your power. And the light of your deeper understanding of things will help cast out the darkness of the world. You will be the same you, but a very different you. Something happened inside you, and you are changed.

The star pointing to the manger where Christ was born is a star that shines within everyone's consciousness, signaling to the mortal mind that there is someplace else to go. We've lingered long enough in the regions of darkness, thinking we are separate from God and from each other. The delusions thereby manufactured are now threatening to destroy us.

As children we learned about evolution. We learned that if a species consistently behaves in maladaptive ways, it will either evolve or it will go extinct. An evolutionary alternative occurs when a mutation happens: a member of the species demonstrates another way of behavior more aligned with a survivable future for the species. Humanity's fear-based behavioral patterns are now so maladaptive that they are a threat to our survival. Humanity's current challenge is to survive itself.

In order to change our behavior, however, we will have to change our minds. The mystic Jesus is a transformer of minds. He is an evolutionary alternative, the self reborn out of darkness and into light.

Mary gave birth to him with all her love. Now it's our turn.

Dear God,
Please use me.
May Your spirit come over me and prepare my heart.
I surrender to You who and what I am,
that I might be a vessel of Your love.
Enter me and lift me up
that I might serve You best.
Amen

Miracles

In the words of Albert Einstein, "We cannot solve our problems with the same level of thinking that created them." There is a quantum field that lies beyond the limits of the world as we understand it. Our rational mind cannot grasp it fully, for it is beyond the understanding of the mortal mind. The heart, however, is totally at home there.

Miracle-mindedness returns the mind to its proper function, which means alignment with and service to love. The Mind of God is an infinite ocean of loving thought, and when we think with love we are thinking with God. The purpose of our lives is to learn to think as God thinks.

Every thought is a cause that leads to an effect; the world is like a screen onto which are projected the nature of our thoughts. The Law of Cause and Effect was created for our protection, for as long as we think with love, then love is reflected back to us.

But that's not what is going on here, at least not usually. Humanity is dominated by a loveless thought system, the ego's playground, emerging from the mistaken thought that we are separate. The belief in separation leads to all manner of chaos.

Like a cancer cell that has disconnected from its collaborative function, our thoughts are prone to separating themselves from their divine purpose. That itself is the essential problem: we've been infected by the malignant thought that "it's all about me." Thinking we are separate, we then consistently attack what and whom we were born to love.

The separation itself is an illusion of consciousness, for on the level of the spirit there's no place where you start and I stop. We're like waves in the ocean thinking we are separate from other waves. Obviously, there is no place where one wave stops and another wave starts. Yet think of the psychological difference between thinking of yourself as a wave that is separate from the rest of the ocean versus thinking of yourself as one with it.

If I think of myself as one wave separate from every other, how can I not feel powerless in relation to the rest of the ocean? How can I not live in constant fear of annihilation, terrified a wave that is bigger than me will overwhelm me at any moment? Why would I not then defend my separateness, believing that without it I will cease to exist?

On the other hand, if I think of myself as one with the other waves, how could I not feel safe and powerful? Identifying with the power of the ocean itself, I have no reason to fear, because I know that I am part of it.

Believing we are separate, yet knowing in our hearts that we are not, we suffer. Our entire existence is a fixed double bind. We are left with no sense of meaning, higher identity, or purpose. The world as we have come to know it—a realm of disordered thoughts, manufactured chaos, and disconnected events—is not who we are, and we cannot feel safe within it.

This is a deadly game, but it is a game we're playing with ourselves. With our loveless thoughts we have concocted a loveless world. In closing our hearts we have blinded our eyes. But God did not do this to us; we did it to ourselves.

There is a way to escape this pain. Yet it's something the ego will not tolerate. Escape lies in surrendering the belief that we are separate, which the ego finds intolerable because the end of the separation is the death of the ego. It becomes vicious in its drive to preserve its life. In its panicked, hysterical drive to perpetuate itself, the ego takes out all the stops to convince us that the separation is real and that our oneness is the illusion. It insists everyone is guilty, even ourselves. It insists we are isolated specks of nothingness afloat in a random, uncaring universe.

How could this not produce a deep and abiding anxiety, routinely suppressed yet always haunting us? And from that place of spiritual ignorance, uninformed of who we are and who we are to each other, we make endlessly foolish decisions. Insisting the separation is real, we look to the material world for comfort when our overidentification with it is the actual source of our discomfort. We build our mental prison, then seek to decorate it with gold.

We use our minds to attack and defend when the purpose of our lives is to love and bless—all this in an unconscious drive to perpetuate the separation that is the engine of our despair. Our thinking upside down, our lives are upside down. Our hearts invalidated, our lives are filled with suffering. Our minds confused, our world is filled with terror.

Ah, but from this insanity we are miraculously saved.

The Separation

The fundamental premise of *A Course in Miracles* is that love is real and nothing else exists. But if only love is real, then why is endless love not our experience as we go through life? If God is love, why would He even allow the ego to exist?

As extensions of the mind of God, we share His attributes. The only difference between us is that He created us; we did not create Him. Free will means we can think whatever it is we wish to think. God Himself will not violate that right.

The thought system that dominates this earth is based on fear, not love. That thought system has extraordinary power because it is the power of the mind turned against itself.

Love is natural to us, yet often feels foreign. From a very early age, natural thinking begins to feel unnatural to us and unnatural thought to feel natural. We live in a world where thoughts of attack, blame, and judgment have become more instinctive to us than love and forgiveness. That is the source of both our personal and our collective despair.

We are constantly tempted by an insane resistance to love. We are driven by a conscious and unconscious opposition to it, and that is the struggle underlying every problem. The spiritual journey is the effort to free ourselves from this mental imprisonment, and Jesus is one of the portals through which we can make our escape. He frees us by reminding us who we are.

Millions of years ago in time as we know it, we thought a thought that was not true—a lie so great that it shattered the universe. We began to think without love. "The opposite of love is fear," says the *Course*. "But what is all-encompassing can have no opposite"* (T-1). When we're thinking without love, we actually aren't thinking at all. Fear is the mortal hallucination of a life lived separately from God. People ask, "But if God is love, then why did He allow the creation of the ego to begin with?" And that's the point. He didn't. The ego is merely a false belief.

That belief was our original misperception, or mis-creation. It began as a moment of disconnection, a separation from love, that is the source of all horror in the world. It was a "detour into fear"* (T-17), described in the *Course* as a moment when the Son of God forgot to laugh. The problem is not that the separation happened millions of years ago; the problem is that we reenact it in any moment that we close our hearts. It is the chronic spiritual sickness of humankind, the endless repetition of unloving thoughts that dominate the world. For the mind is so powerful that what we think, we manifest. There is only one problem, and there is only one solution. We think we have many different problems, but we really only have one: our separation from love.

The original moment of loveless thought was the birth of the ego (the word used here the way it was used by the ancient Greeks: the notion of a small, separated self). The ego is only a *belief* that we are separate, yet belief is very powerful. From that one false belief an entire world of lovelessness came into being.

Two separate worlds, like two parallel universes, would from that moment coexist.

One world is peopled by separate bodies who have forgotten who we are and forgotten we are one with each other. Our bodies are physical manifestations of the thought that we are separate. Freud defined neurosis as "separation from self." We perceive this world with our physical senses: our eyes see, our ears hear, our hands touch. But while the physical world is real within our three dimensions, three-dimensional reality itself is not what it appears to be. It is but a vast matrix of illusion manufactured by the human mind, not to illuminate but in fact to hide a world that lies beyond it.

A parallel world, unseen by the physical eye, is an eternal indestructible reality. It is God's ocean of endless light, love, and understanding, eclipsed by the ego's thought system that now dominates the world.

We straddle two universes, attached to one while yearning for the other. We live in a world of separate bodies, on a hamster's wheel of fear-based thought and behavior, perversely guided by the false belief that our separateness is our identity, without which we cease to exist.

The thought that we are separate has led us to believe that we are separate from God, separate from each other, separate from the universe, separate from the earth, separate from the animals, even separate from ourselves. This thought system violates and invalidates, torments and destroys us, making us mental slaves to its dictatorial insistence that we're not who we are and that we are who we are not.

Beyond all that is our spiritual Reality. It is the indestructible realm that God created, within which we are one and where our souls know that we're at home.

The Holy Spirit

So here we have been, lost in the illusion of separateness, experiencing ourselves as alone in a meaningless universe when we
ourselves are its meaning. Literally from the beginning of time,
we have enacted and reenacted the drama created by this first
mistaken thought.

God, being perfect Love, has the answer to every problem the
moment the problem occurs. The ego having responded to God,
God responded right back. Into the darkness there appeared a
light.

What would perfect Love do, in response to the fact that we
had opposed it? Would it force us back to the thought of love?
No, because Love does not force.

Would it punish us for thinking without love? No, because
Love does not punish.

God wouldn't force us to return our minds to love, for that
would be a violation of our free will. We are free to think whatever we choose to think. But in the instant the ego appeared, God
created an Alternative, a place in our consciousness that would
guide us back to love should we so choose.

This guide, a gentle bridge of perception from fear to love, is called, among other things, the Holy Spirit.

The Holy Spirit is the eternal communication link between us and God, the reconnecting link to our right mind. Created by God, the Holy Spirit is therefore eternal and will remain in our minds forever. The Holy Spirit also goes by the name of Internal Teacher, Comforter, Shekhinah, Thought Adjuster, and more. From the Holy Spirit comes God's greatest gift: a flood of loving thought with the power to override our fearful perceptions and bring us inner peace. Jesus was, and is, a manifestation of the Holy Spirit.

Fear is to love what darkness is to light, not a thing but the absence of a thing. Just as we get rid of darkness by turning on the light, we get rid of fear by replacing it with love. Fear is the darkness of the mind; the Holy Spirit, the Light of the World.

While the Holy Spirit was created literally millions of years ago, there lived a man two thousand years ago (the *Course* says he is not the only one) who actualized the mind of the Holy Spirit, eliminating from his consciousness all thoughts but those of love. He thus became one with the Holy Spirit, and to call on one is to call on the other. He is the light in the presence of which darkness cannot be.

This light has many names, and Jesus is one. The mystic Jesus is a purveyor of the Holy Spirit, a way of calling down the Holy Spirit's power within our mortal existence. We do not see Him with our physical eyes, but we see the effects of His power and we know that He is there.

Jesus cannot save us from the effects of our thinking, for the Law of Cause and Effect was created by God for our protection and is therefore inviolable. He works with us on the causal level, helping us to choose our thoughts more wisely.

Every instant we choose what to think, either consciously or unconsciously. Thoughts of love bring inner peace, because when we think with love we are *being ourselves*. Thinking without love, we are nullifying our own existence. The awareness of our oneness is heaven and the torment of the ego is hell—not places we go to after we die, but emotional states right here right now.

God doesn't send us to hell; He is What delivers us from it. All of us are tempted at times to deviate from love, just as Jesus was. Through the grace of God he rose above the temptation. Now he is authorized to help us rise above ours.

All of us have days when for whatever reason we're discombobulated. In today's world, things are moving at an unnaturally quick pace. While it wasn't very long ago that our ancestors lived their lives according to the rising and setting of the sun, today's social media environment seems to have quickened time itself. Our nervous systems literally were not made for this. Of course we are tempted. Of course we fall.

Our civilization needs repair. *We* need repair. We cannot simply numb or suppress the pain of living in a world so at odds with who we are. The world is going to have to change; civilization is going to have to correct its course. But for any of that to happen, we're going to have to change ourselves first.

The Atonement

The Atonement is the correction of our perception, placed within us by God as an eternal escape route from fear. Through the Atonement, we can undo the consequences of our loveless-ness, as we recognize our errors and ask God's help in choosing another way to think. All Abrahamic religions, as well as others, contain the principle of Atonement, for it is fundamental to personal and collective transformation. We cannot go forward in life without correcting our hearts, and this is as true for a nation and a species as it is for an individual. The Atonement, empowered by nothing short of the infinite love and the power of God, bestows upon us full release from the insanity of the world we have created, and deliverance to the one that He did.

The Atonement, however, takes more than a simple "Oops, I shouldn't have done that." Any Catholic in sincere confession, or Jew in tears on Yom Kippur, or addict at an Alcoholics Anonymous meeting, admitting the exact nature of their wrongs, has touched the zone of deep contrition where we recognize we have transgressed and we wish to transgress no more.

When we do, something genuinely miraculous happens.

Something changes on a causal level. We fall to our knees, if not literally then figuratively. And everything begins again.

That is where the world is now, or perhaps it is truer to say it's where we need to be now: not attacking others, blaming others, playing victim, or making the problem about someone else. We need to look within ourselves for the problem, and within ourselves for the answers. We need to forgive ourselves and others. For that is where God is, and that is where the Answer lies.

The Atonement principle heals every heart that is open to it. When we are willing to go back to the moment when the mistake was made, to take full responsibility for the fact that in that moment we did not allow the Holy Spirit to guide our perceptions and our behavior, we can choose again. We can put the moment into the hands of the Holy Spirit now. And we need not feel guilty, for He will undo all consequences of our wrong decision if we will let Him. The Atonement principle does not come from us, but it is within us because God put it there.

When fear occurs—a repetition of the original moment of separation—the universe is always ready to correct itself. The question is whether we are. All of us fall off the spiritual wagon more times a day than we care to admit. But at any given moment, we can choose again. That is the power of the Atonement.

In the moment when we close our hearts, choosing fear instead of love, the miracle we could have had is held in trust for us by the Holy Spirit. It will be safe in His hands until we are ready to receive it. It might be another situation, at another time, but the opportunity will be provided. The miracle available to us in any moment is an undeletable file. We can choose not to download it, but we can never remove it from the hard drive.

In the presence of perfect love, the universe rearranges itself and miracles occur automatically. That is the infinite mercy of God.

Enlightenment

For thousands of years, both Jews and Christians have conceived of a Messiah who liberates humanity from spiritual and material bondage. The Jews say the Messiah is coming, the Christians say the Messiah came, and Einstein said there is no time.

The mystic Messiah won't be coming from outside but from the inside. He's not coming down from the sky; he's coming from our higher mind.

Thinking of the Messiah only in terms of linear time and the historical reality of Jesus keeps us bound to limited awareness. The mystic Messiah is a state of mind, a loving awareness of our oneness with God and with each other. In that sense the Messiah does liberate the children of God.

But liberation is not a moment, it's a process. Time and space, and the body itself, are learning devices through which we rehearse over and over again the lessons of enlightenment. Every circumstance is carefully planned by the Holy Spirit for our maximal soul growth, both challenging and inviting us to choose love instead of fear.

Enlightenment isn't a change in our bodies but in our souls, not a denial of the body but a rethinking of its purpose. God honors our creations as we are asked to honor His. Nothing in this world is holy or unholy except as determined by the purpose we ascribe to it. The body itself is like a priceless suit of clothes. Used as a means of healing and communication, it too is a holy thing.

In many Christian churches you'll see it written: "Do this in remembrance of me." The mind of Jesus holds nothing but faith, nothing but love, and nothing but service. In every situation, our spiritual challenge is to even try to approach that.

It's quite a task to go over the events of our lives at the end of each day, asking, "In that situation, did I bring forth my best? Did I show love and generosity, or fear and selfishness? Was I there to give, or was I there to take? Did I bless, or did I blame?" It's amazing how the more we do this, the more we begin to see that our lives are exactly as we program them with our thoughts.

We're not asked by God to be perfect, but to be honest. Every time we realize "Yep, I wasn't my best in that instance," we can place that moment into the hands of God, atone for our error, and pray for the chance to begin again. He will provide it. That is the power of the Atonement. It isn't a fix; it's a miracle.

The choice for love is a radical departure from the way we've been taught to view the world. Enlightenment is a psychological conversion that ultimately dismantles a thought system based on fear, but not without temptation and hardships that every life is privy to.

The temptations of the ego are pernicious. How often we self-sabotage, only to realize afterward that we ourselves were the enemy who hurt us most. The ego would much prefer that you monitor the faults of others than to be honest about your own. Yet it's only when we're willing to look at ourselves clearly in the mirror that the path of liberation begins.

Enlightenment isn't a stupendous moment after which everything is suddenly clear and we're forever changed. It's a moment-by-moment, often arduous process of personal growth that can involve, and in fact usually does involve, some level of personal discomfort. Growth is messy. The journey is scary, and a guide—a friend to support us as we go, solidly there with us and never to leave, that and more—is the mystic Jesus.

He overshadows our consciousness, delivering us to thinking that will set us free of pain. The purpose of our lives is to be happy, and the only way we can achieve that is if we learn to think as God thinks. Asking Jesus to help us is a way to get there. There is a mystery to what happens when we invite him into our heart, something beyond the grasp of our mortal mind.

The *Course* refers to our relationship to him: "⁶It is possible to read his words and benefit from them without accepting him into your life. ⁷Yet he would help you yet a little more if you will share your pains and joys with him, and leave them both to find the peace of God"* (MT-88). I have found that to be true.

Giving up how we used to think means giving up who we used to be, and the old self rarely goes down easily. The journey takes us through a very dark forest, filled with psychological demons that jump out at us as we seek to make our way: thoughts of past failures, personal humiliation, shame, self-hatred, regret, and grief.

The mystic path is an insistence on meaning in an otherwise meaningless universe, a dedication to purpose in a world that constantly distracts us with seduction by ultimately unimportant things. It is a refusal to go along with the corrupting influence of petty judgments. It is a commitment to making forgiveness the core principle around which we live our lives.

There is so much to unlearn. The temptation to perceive without love—choosing attack over forgiveness and blame over blessing—is more than the dominant norm in our world; it's the *preferred* one. And it will challenge us at every turn.

Years ago, I told myself not to worry about the devil because that was only in my head. I remember the moment I realized that that is hardly good news. The devil isn't out there somewhere stalking the planet for men's souls. Rather, it is the temptation in all of us, ever vigilant and ever active, to perceive without love. Since all minds are one, as we transcend that temptation within ourselves, we help purify the thoughts of the world.

We'll be forced by circumstances to see where we are spiritually strong and where we are spiritually weak. The Holy Spirit isn't here to honor our comfort zones but to bust them, to bring to our awareness the places where we still hold love at bay. Only then can we atone for those aspects of our personality and heal from them.

Just as we mentally exercise to build our physical muscles, we exercise to build our spiritual muscles. Jesus is like a great trainer, going through the moves with us, correcting us when we didn't quite get it right, helping us develop greater strength with which to do it for ourselves. Yoga or Pilates or weight training changes the shape of our physical muscles; a consistent effort to be more loving changes the shape of our personality. By disciplining ourselves to be more loving, we don't just become "nicer." We become miracle workers, healers, and agents of transformation. That is why we are here.

As there are objective, discernible laws of physics, there are objective, discernible laws of consciousness, or metaphysics, as well. You don't have "faith" in the power of gravity; you simply understand the power of gravity. At a certain point you don't have faith in the power of love either; you simply understand the power of love.

If we're confused, or angry, or intolerant, or triggered, God does not ask us not to be. He simply asks us to be *willing* not to be. Knowing there is a power that can do for us what we cannot do for ourselves at that moment, knowing there is within our mind a savior from our confusion and despair, it's up to us whether we choose to call on it. Jesus can't come into our mind and simply take those things from us—he can't take what we don't release to him—but if we request his help we will receive it.

Part of the art of life is not doing something stupid in the meantime. Just as physical exercise builds physical muscles, prayer and meditation build attitudinal muscles. One gives us the strength to move quickly and powerfully. The other gives us the strength to remain nonreactive and still. I might think you're the biggest jerk in the world right now—I might not yet be beyond thinking that—but with enough practice, I can get myself to the point where I'm not dumb enough to text you that.

Every action has a reaction, and every thought takes form on some level. "A neutral thought is impossible"* (WB-26). A miracle is a fundamental correction on the causal level of thought. It is useless to try to change our lives by simply tinkering with its effects. That's like trying to change the plot of a movie by manipulating the screen. Everything we experience in life is simply the projection of a thought.

The shift from fear to love is literally a transformation of worlds; it's a change on the causal level of existence that then changes the realm of effects. God Himself will not violate the Law of Cause and Effect because His creations are unalterable. The mystic Jesus transforms our lives by transforming how we think. As humanity changes our thinking, the world will miraculously change.

How often our appetites, our reactivity, our lack of impulse control, our anger, our defensiveness, our fear get in the way of our good. It can take more than garden-variety "positive think-ing" to get past all that. Perhaps we were betrayed, or injured, or abandoned, or lied to. Perhaps we lost a loved one, or we know that we or someone close to us is dying. Of course we're think-ing angry, negative, or desperate thoughts. It's not always easy to change our mind. Life can be painful and depressing. It's easy enough to love when the love around us is obvious—when we're being treated kindly; when we feel loved; when circumstances are going well.

The difficulty sets in when things are not going well; when we do not feel loved; when circumstances are not as we'd wish. That's when the ego is very good at convincing us all this love and forgiveness is pure nonsense, not to be believed, or acted on, or taken seriously in any way.

Jesus transforms all that by transforming our mind. That's the same thing as saying he is the light that dissolves the darkness.

To "follow Jesus" means to align our thoughts with uncon-ditional love. In him there are no conditions, no excuses, no il-lusions that stand in the way of his love. In him, therefore, our illusions of separation disappear. As we become his disciples, our minds become more disciplined.

We achieve too little because we have undisciplined minds. All of us have those areas of life where we are wounded—places in ourselves where, usually because of some drama that occurred in the past, the muscles of our personality have become misshapen. We're weak where we might be stronger, if we'd had different parents. We're harsh where we might be gentle, had we not been abused. We're negative where we might be more positive, had we not been betrayed or hurt. The sum of our accumulated wound-ings, from birth until this moment, takes a toll on our emotional body. We carry internal scars and bruises, the emotional wounds that have never healed. It's one thing to come to see those wounds; it's another thing to heal them.

All of us are privy to the darkness of the world, and carry it within ourselves. A traditional psychotherapeutic approach involves analyzing the darkness, while praying for a miracle means turning on the light. The Light of the World is a light in your mind. He has risen, and so can we.

Dear God,
Please make me who You would have me be
that I might do as You would have me do.
Transform my mind and heal my heart.
Release me from torment
that I might help release others.
Show me my innocence
that I might more clearly see theirs.
Bless me that my life might be a blessing on the world.
May love and love only be my way, dear God.
Amen

CHAPTER TWO

REFLECTIONS OF LIGHT

P EOPLE CAN HAVE an almost pathological need to "make something of themselves," as though who they are already simply
isn't enough.

To the ego, you will never be enough. It doesn't tell you that
you did something wrong; it just tells you that you *are* wrong.
Few of us, no matter how kind our parents or how healthy our
upbringing, survive into adulthood without an arsenal of rockets
in our head shouting us down before anyone else has a chance to.

That's why knowing who you are spiritually is essential to a
healthy sense of self. If we only accept the world's estimation,
then we'll never feel like we're enough, because the world is dominated by the ego's vicious nonsense. If we accept ourselves as
God created us, we recognize we're no better and no worse than
anyone else. All of us are special, and none of us is special. At
the deepest level of our spiritual identity, all of us are perfect creations of God.

Central to understanding this is recognizing where we came
from. *A Course in Miracles* says we have an authorship problem.

We seem to think we authored ourselves, which if you think about it is incredibly arrogant. Or we think we were created by our parents, a sperm and egg apparently carrying magical powers to produce feelings, hopes, great art, and an ultimate yearning for transcendence.

The mortal you is a result of your parents having sex, of course, and your mortal personality is in many ways a result of how your parents behaved since the moment you were born. But none of that is the Real you. Your worldly parents parented your worldly self, but God is the parent of who you really are. We have always lived in Him, and we will always live in Him. Our problem is when we fail to individuate from our parents, yet individuate too much from God.

The ego is like an impostor, a veil, a wall made of broken shards of glass behind which lies an endless field of roses. It's a mask we wear that convinces not only others, but even ourselves, that this impostor is who we are. But *you* are not a body, *you* are not your personality, and *you* are not the mere sum of your human experiences. You are something so infinitely, magnificently beyond all that, and all your deep grief is you longing to be you.

There are many ways to express all this, none better or worse than any other. God is loving thought, and you are an extension of that thought. God is loving cause, and you are its effect. God is Father, and you are His beloved child. Jesus is someone who actualized all that, and in identifying with him you begin to identify yourself.

Apocalyptic Beginnings

When I look back over the span of my life, I sum it up pretty much like this: "It could have gone either way."

I've met so many people living in dire circumstances I know could have been mine. One different turn here or stupid choice there, and it could be me spending years in prison, addicted, on the streets, or even dead. I've been up close and personal with some of the deepest suffering, and I know that there but for the grace of God go I.

I was a bit wild when I was young, and I had many opportunities to self-destruct. The fact that I barely escaped disaster delivered a very powerful message to me: to spend the rest of my life doing whatever I could to persuade others not to be as stupid as I had been. To take life more seriously. To be more responsible toward myself and others. To try my best to be the woman God would have me be.

This isn't some goody-goody mentality. It's simply the gratitude and praise that millions of us feel, knowing that something bigger than ourselves delivered us from the lowest rings of hell. A lot of good things come out of that too, including the development of emotional antibodies of some kind. Once you've seen the worst, when you see it again you're not so scared.

Ironically, that this is true for so many people is one of the most hopeful things happening in our world today. It means we're ready for what comes next. While many traditional Christians believe we face the Apocalypse up ahead, after which there will be a thousand years of peace, the mystic reads that chapter of the Bible differently.

A lot of us have already experienced our personal apocalypse. For some it was the diagnosis of cancer. For some it was getting sober. For some it was unutterable loss. For some it was bankruptcy. For some it was divorce. And from the experience, we have grown more wise. Just as Jesus would appear during those thousand years of peace, in a way he has appeared to us. And each of us now carries a piece of the wisdom that, when combined with the wisdom of others, can and will save the world in time.

Either that, or it's absolutely within the realm of possibility that we could bring about a global apocalypse. It's not up to us what we learn, but only whether we learn through joy or through pain. If we choose not to be wise, we might blow up the world. If enough of us choose to follow the wisdom we've gained from living life so far, then we will avoid a global calamity and go straight for global peace.

In both of those scenarios, Jesus is standing there when the apocalypse is over. In a mystical interpretation he is with us now, showing us how to bypass the darkness and go directly for the light. He has already transcended. Now so can we.

The Power of the Morning

Ilook at morning prayer and meditation the way I look at physical exercise. If I do it, it works. It takes work to strengthen our attitudinal muscles, just as it takes work to strengthen our physical muscles. We use spiritual exercise to counter the emotional gravity of victimization and anger, shame and self-hatred, the way we counter physical gravity by working out. The mystic Jesus is like a spiritual trainer. He can't do the work *for* you, but he can show you how to do it for yourself.

There's no better time to do it than in the morning.

When I was pregnant with my daughter many years ago, I could feel how much was going on inside me as I simply sat on a chair with my feet up drinking a cup of chamomile tea. I was in awe of the thought that new life was being created inside my body. The greatest way I could serve the process was to cultivate health and stillness and inner peace, for myself and for the child within me.

Now I'm similarly in awe of the life that gestates in the womb of consciousness. Sometimes the greatest service I could offer to the child in my womb was to sit quietly and merely be; a life that's pregnant with greater awareness is similarly grounded in stillness and rest. Inner peace is a fertile field for the birth of the mystic self. It is also its ultimate goal.

Giving birth to another human being, but also giving birth to a higher version of ourselves, means we're participating in the birth of a new world. While the species can't continue unless enough of us conceive children, it won't survive unless we conceive enough wisdom.

The effort to become more spiritually conscious involves changes on both the inner and outer planes. In the words of Martin Luther King Jr., we need "qualitative shifts in our souls as well as quantitative changes in our circumstances." Some of those changes are lifestyle changes, one of which involves the earliest hours of our day. All great religious traditions emphasize the importance of the morning.

When we first awaken, our minds are most open to new impressions. That's when we download the state of consciousness that will dominate our day. We have a sacred responsibility to ourselves to choose wisely what that download will be; if we go straight to social media, for instance, rather than going first to God, it's like eating a bowl of candy for breakfast. Your body doesn't want that, and your mind doesn't want it either.

Morning should be sacred, a time when we ground ourselves in a reverent view of ourselves, our relationships, and the world around us. It's a time to consciously call in the light so darkness won't overwhelm us. Particularly given the chaos in the world today, acquiescing to the ego's worldview first thing in the morning is one of the most self-sabotaging things we can do.

We do not need to create the world; it has already been created and created perfectly. Our problem is our attachment to an unreal world that lies in front of it.

The world on this side of the veil is the ego's kingdom, in which thoughts of fear and limitation prevail. Through the eyes of the Holy Spirit, we gain the power to see beyond the veil. Withdrawing our attachment to one world, we gain the ability to invoke another. Beyond this world is a world we want* (WB-235).

It's ours to decide which realm of reality we wish to show on the big screen that takes up space in our mind. But according to *A Course in Miracles* the vision of one world will cost us the vision of the other. Grounding ourselves in peace and stillness, love and forgiveness, in the morning is one of the most powerful medicines we can apply to our wounded souls. Spiritual liberation is not a bursting out, but a gentle melting in. The mystic Jesus is the tender power at the core of who we are, and the protector of the mystic mind.

We wake up in the morning and take a shower or bath in order to wash dirt off our body. We want to wash ourselves clean of physical impurities left over from the day before. Through meditation, prayer, mindfulness, or whatever spiritual practice we follow, we do the same thing with our mind. We take a shower to wash away the dirt that has accumulated on our body, and we meditate and pray in order to wash away the stress that has accumulated on our mind.

It's not just our intellect that is assaulted by the fear and chaos of the world today: our *nervous system* is assaulted by it. And that weakens our capacity to be effective in the world. We can't bring peace to the world around us if we ourselves are not at peace. We're not going to change the world if we ourselves remain unchanged. "Do not conform to the pattern of this world, but be transformed by the renewing of your mind" (Romans 12:2, New International Version).

That's why prayer and meditation matter. Meditation is a scientifically proven process that shifts our brain waves, leading to chemical changes in the brain that cause a deep experience of inner peace.

Time spent meditating removes the mental plaque that accumulates on our psyche—the layers of ego thinking that cover over our miracle impulses and make access to the higher mind impossible. According to A Course of Miracles, five minutes spent with the Holy Spirit in the morning guarantees He will be in charge of our thought forms throughout the day. Simply sitting, reading inspirational or scriptural material, following a serious prayer or meditation practice, we allow our mind to be in a receptive mode to something higher than ourselves. It transforms our experience of life.

The ego's resistance to a quiet moment can be very strong, of course; it loves to make a direct beeline for our adrenal system, addict us to fearful thinking, and destroy all impulse control. There are times when it takes more emotional discipline to be quiet and do nothing than it does to send a reactive text. That's why one of the most undermining things we can do is check email, Instagram, Twitter, and so forth before we meditate in the morning. Just as we train our physical muscles to help us move powerfully, we train our spiritual muscles to help us be powerfully nonreactive and still.

Being a mother myself, I know how many young parents are saying to themselves as you read this, "Oh, but mornings are impossible! She doesn't understand what it's like having little kids around!" But yes, I do. And this is what I learned: small children love it when we say very softly, "Hey, now we're going to have our quiet time with God, okay? We're going to sit here with each other and just love Him!" I cannot stress how important it is to help small children get used to spiritual practice. Try to do it early. Once the eye-rolling years begin, it's almost impossible.

Nothing would do more to repair the damage to our families than to cultivate quiet among ourselves. The French philosopher Blaise Pascal said that every problem in the world can be traced to man's inability to sit quietly in a room alone. In both Judaism and Christianity, there is the notion of the small, still voice within, but that voice is easily drowned out by the cacophonous noises of the world.

If we do not fill our minds in the morning with the light of a higher love, the darkness of the world will have its way with us. Our mental energy is going to go somewhere, and if we don't proactively direct it, devote it, and surrender it to love, then it will be used for the purposes of fear. And of course, that jangles us. Our only two real choices today are between enlightenment or neurosis.

If you've chosen a prayer or meditation practice that feels right to you, try adding this every morning: Close your eyes, visualize everyone you're going to meet in the day ahead of you, imagine everyone you don't even know you're going to meet, and simply send love from your heart to theirs. See Jesus embrace them, along with whatever other imagery emerges.

We are far too tolerant of mind-wandering* (T-29), casually traveling the back alleys of fear and meaninglessness that pervade the world today. We need to consciously, routinely quiet our minds if we wish to hear the Voice for God. The mystic Jesus will speak to us, but it's our responsibility to develop the habit of listening. Yes, that means turning off television and iPads during dinner. Yes, it means pulling ourselves away from addictive patterns of thought and behavior. And it definitely means knowing when to put the phone down.

None of this is always easy, but we can at least lean into the changes that foster our rebirth. Even small changes can have profound results. And always remember, the mystic Jesus will help you. See yourself taking his hand as a child would take the hand of an Elder Brother. He will help you. Think of him in order to remove the veil before your eyes, to see beyond appearances, to penetrate the layers of illusion that otherwise dominate your mind.

As part of your daily spiritual practice, this morning prayer from *A Course in Miracles* is a powerful directive to your subconscious mind to do the bidding of the Holy Spirit:

> *Where would you have me go?*
> *What would you have me do?*
> *What would you have me say, and to whom?* (WB-122)

Then, as the day winds down, a powerful way to bring the mind to rest is with an honest appraisal of how we did that day.

Whom do I need to forgive?

Where was I not my most loving? Is there anything I need to correct?

What was the part I played in whatever problem plagued me?

Is there anyone I owe an apology?

Where did I indulge the habit of negativity and blame?

Where was I holding on to the past?

With each one, simply look at it, forgive yourself and others, place it all in the hands of God and be at peace. If there's something you need to do as a follow-up, you'll know.

There is something about the word "Jesus" that automatically reminds the mind of something. It's not that the name itself carries magical power. It's that the brain responds to the name in some way, like a medicine for the subconscious mind.

If a problem seems insurmountable, try closing your eyes and see Jesus walking on water. If you lack faith that a situation can miraculously change, see him turning water into wine. If you're acting in service but you lack the resources you need, see him multiplying the loaves and fishes. If you feel afraid, reach out for his hand and he will guide you. For mystic Jesus is the mind of pure love, and perfect love casts out fear.

If you're having a difficult time in a relationship, see him embracing you both. Before you go into a meeting, bless everyone in the room. Pray silently to be a vessel of love, pray that the Holy Spirit pour forth His spirit on the gathering, and ask Him to use you to help heal the world. Pray to see and appreciate the value of everyone who is gathered. See Jesus with his arms around everyone; see him sitting at a conference table where you're having an important meeting; see him embracing everyone involved if you're having a difficult conversation.

None of those visions are idle fantasies.

If you treat this kind of imagery like a toy, it will have the effect of a toy in your life. But if you treat it like the power of the universe, so shall it be for you. There is nothing in the world more powerful than your ability to use your mind to glorify God. Not by saying His name out loud or proselytizing for your religion, but simply by being the person that you know He would have you be. "Teach the gospel" means "demonstrate love."

Because all minds are joined, everyone subconsciously knows everything. People you meet today won't consciously know they've been blessed by you, but they will feel it. They won't know exactly why they like you so much.

They simply will.

Being Saved

The mystic Jesus repudiates and dissolves the power of the ego. He teaches us how to love in a world where it can often be so hard.

The birth of the mystic self is a commitment to becoming who we are capable of being, a willingness to die to who we used to be in order to become who we are capable of being. "He that findeth his life shall lose it: and he that loseth his life for my sake shall find it" (Matthew 10:39, KJV).

Spiritual rebirth isn't an easy way out; it's more like a difficult way in. And we often run away from such work. We prefer the dull ache of unconscious living to the sharp pains of self-discovery.

Pulling an entire thought system out by its roots is not an easy thing to do. We've been taught since childhood to see ourselves as separate from others; we've been taught that the world is dangerous, that there are only so many pieces of the pie to go around, that no one is good enough, particularly ourselves, and so forth. We've been taught in many ways that toughness is strength and gentleness is weakness, only to learn the hard way that controlling behavior can turn people off and humility draws them in. We were taught that self-will is everything and grace is just a fantasy, when in fact self-will is often self-sabotaging, and the experience of grace nothing short of miraculous.

In a world where we are taught to fear, however, we can train ourselves to think differently. Imagine if you had a kind of internal coach, with you all the time, a Teacher who would take each thought you gave to him and show you how to uplift it. Who would show you how to love yourself, and how to love others. Who would guide you in the ways of forgiveness. That is who Jesus is.

If Shakespeare dropped by and said he would teach you how to write better, would you turn down his offer? If Picasso dropped by and offered to teach you to paint, would you turn down the offer? That's what Jesus does, in a way: he makes us an offer—to teach us how to think more clearly, love more deeply, live more creatively, and so save humanity from itself. Once you realize it's an offer like that—just that simple, really, with no strings attached—it makes you think a bit before you refuse.

The only thing we need to be "saved" from is our own fear-based thinking. Yet fear often masquerades as something it is not: sophisticated thought, demanding that we bow down to its authority. Self-hate can masquerade as self-love, selfishness can masquerade as self-care, and casting a brother out of our hearts can masquerade as having healthy boundaries. The last thing fear would want us to do is to see that we ourselves are the main source of our problems.

The Holy Spirit stands on the fence between the self eternally at peace with God and the self that is lost in the egoic confusion of the world. He sees you as you really are, and He sees your worldly personality. Most significantly, He sees and understands the gap between the two.

We turn to our Internal Teacher to transform our thoughts, so that even in this world we can experience the truth of who we are.

We do so by handing Him every thought that comes to mind, asking that He remove the elements of illusion, of fear, and give our thoughts back to us transformed.

An example would be this: There is someone in your life who treats you in a way that is unkind, unloving, or disrespectful. In response, you are triggered in various ways, based on childhood wounds or any other factor. Your temptation is then to close your heart to them—judgment, defensiveness, and so forth—as they have closed their heart to you.

The ego would have you see yourself as victim, filled with righteous anger and totally justified in defending or attacking back in some way. Defense itself is an attack, however, and now both of you have jumped onto the wheel of suffering. And the initial offense might have been anything. It could have been a serious transgression or even something as simple as an unkind remark on Twitter. Even small annoyances, accumulated over time, have the capacity to leave us anxious, devitalized, and depressed. A rampant mean-spiritedness begins to express itself collectively, as an entire society can feel itself subject to often subtle, sometimes dramatic expressions of lovelessness that begin to fill the air.

But there is another way. The journey begins in the realm of personal transformation, and over time has societal effects. In praying for ourselves we are praying for the world.

Dear God,
I am annoyed and hurt by _____'s behavior.
Their lovelessness has triggered me and I am not at peace.
I give to you the feelings I feel,
asking that you transform them.

Reflections of Light

I am willing to feel otherwise.
I am willing to see this situation differently.
Please show me the innocence in this person
and myself, that I might be at peace.
Amen

Prayer changes us on the level of cause. Effects of that change automatically follow.

Every thought is either love or fear. All negative thought is an expression of fear. There is really only one problem (fear), and there is really only one Answer (love).

Love is our natural state, yet we're thrown off our natural state as a result of simply living in this world. That is the spiritual meaning of Adam and Eve exiting the garden. All of us, including the person who treated you unkindly, has been wounded by the world. Whereas the love of God is meant to flow into us and extend through us, our woundedness forms an obstruction to our ability to allow that. Ego is when the wires get crossed in our brains: in any moment, for whatever reason, we can't see how to express our love and still get our needs met. We become stuck in that moment and fall asleep to who we are.

That is what happened inside the person who hurt you. They fell asleep to who they are; and in that state, they fell asleep to who you are too. Yet the bigger problem is what happens now. Someone else having fallen asleep to who they are, and to who you are, the temptation is for you to fall asleep too. Your mission—and your miracle—is to remain awake.

You can extend your perception beyond the realm of someone's mistaken, loveless behavior, and choose instead to see their innocence. You can be willing to remember what in your heart you know: that they are an innocent child of God, just like you, and their behavior doesn't have to be perceived as an attack. It is merely a bad dream, and you don't have to enter into it. Their behavior can be seen differently; what is not love can be seen as a call for love.

That does not mean the other person isn't to be held accountable. It doesn't mean there isn't a conversation to be had. It doesn't mean you're to surrender to unhealthy patterns of behavior related to them. Forgiveness simply means you are lifted to a higher mental vibration, from which—and only from which—you will be able to express your yes, and express your no, from a place that is nonreactive and responsible. And, by remaining awake, you will help awaken the other person too.

We are heir to the laws of the world with which we identify. If I choose to perceive your guilt as real, then the effects of it will be real for me. Forgiveness frees us from those effects. If I'm willing to see past your guilt to the innocence beyond, I am freed from the effects of it. In freeing someone else, we free ourselves. Recognizing that in an ultimate sense only love is real, only love then has an effect on us.

Forgiveness then resets the trajectory of a relationship. It pierces the veil and delivers us to oneness. It is the miracle that sets us free.

It's at this point that people might start telling you you're in *denial*.

"No," they'll say, "it *did* happen! And you have every right to be angry!"

Of course you have a right to be angry; you have a right to feel whatever you feel. But no, you don't *need* to be angry. What you need to be is aware.

Following the mystic Jesus doesn't make you any less psychologically astute. Nothing could be more psychologically sophisticated than to recognize how to navigate the deepest regions of the mind. And that's what spirit is: the deepest region of the mind.

Choosing to extend your perception beyond someone's guilt isn't negative denial; it's *positive* denial. You're not denying that something happened, you're simply denying its power over you. You're not looking away from something; you're looking through it, and past it. You're extending your perception into the light that will dissolve the effects of darkness.

Many people these days are aware of the concept of the "spiritual bypass," the idea that we're pouring pink paint over an issue and simply pretending it doesn't exist. That means we skip the important step of owning our pain. That would indeed be negative denial.

But that's not what we're talking about here. In fact, if anything we're talking about becoming even *more* attuned to our feelings—feelings such as anger, shame, humiliation, embarrassment, rejection, and self-hatred. We're just not kidding ourselves that by analyzing them we'll necessarily dissolve the feelings, or that we have the power to simply tell those things to go away. Rather, we bring them up in order to surrender them. Spiritual detox works much like a physical detox; things must come up in order to be released. Jesus cannot take from us what we won't release to him. We say, "This is how I'm feeling, but I am willing to see this differently." That's a more powerful way of shifting our emotions than simply telling them to go away.

And it's when the miracle happens: not just when we "let go," but when we release something into the hands of God. We're willing to see the love that lies beyond the pain, whether it was love we weren't shown or simply love we didn't know how to receive.

The altar to God is in our minds, and to put something on the altar means to put our thoughts about it on the altar. What we put on the altar is then altered. We're willing to see something differently. We're willing for our thoughts to be lifted. And when they are, we at last find peace.

The Destination of
Enlightenment

Imagine if, from the moment you were born, everyone who had ever met you and everything that had ever happened to you had been ten on a scale of one to ten in terms of compassion, mercy, and love. Think who you would be today if that had been your experience.

Now think who you are instead. Think of the places where your emotional reactions are constricted by fear, where you lack trust or self-confidence or a positive outlook. These are places not where you're bad, but where you're wounded. Yet our wounds do not necessarily look like wounds to other people; they're more likely to appear as character defects that only set us up for further pain.

All of us have character defects, of course. But salvation lies in our willingness to change the way we are, not in the endless analysis about why we are the way we are. At a certain point, you don't keep trying to understand why you're needy, negative, controlling, or manipulative. You simply realize you are, admit you are, and ask God to change you.

Dear God,
I know I am harsh where I would be gentle, weak where I
should be strong, judgmental where I should be merciful.
I am willing to change.
Please show me how.
Amen

Scan your personality as though you are looking at yourself from above. See how you manifest to the world, and ask yourself honestly how you come across to others. Reflect on the fact that the life you're living is a result of the person you've become.

Who we are in the world is based on moment-by-moment decisions. Every moment we decide, consciously or unconsciously, whether to face life with an open or closed heart. Whether to embrace the innocence in others and express lovingly, or to constrict in defensiveness, judgment, and unprocessed pain. Fake it till you make it means practice till it's real. And what we find when we do something like that is that doing something *makes* it real.

I have a friend named Kathy who comes from Georgia, and she has a way of addressing almost all her friends as "My love." One day I decided to do that too, and it was amazing the changes I felt as I did. Coming from Texas, I was already big on calling people "Darling"—sort of longish for the "Darlin'" I had grown up around—but "My love" took things to another place. I don't know if I've kept it up, but I know I felt a shift when I did it. It's hard to snap at someone when you're calling them "My love."

Words are not just an expression of thought; they also create thought. And every thought we think takes us, and those around us, straight to heaven or straight to hell. According to *A Course in Miracles*, heaven isn't a condition or a place, but an awareness of our oneness. And hell is the state of anxiety that results when we feel separate from others. Neither happen after we die; they happen in any moment. Every thought takes us in some way closer to the awareness of our oneness or to the anxiety of feeling separate and alone. Again, this isn't about what we get from others. We only get what we choose to give away.

Deciding who we choose to *be* in any moment is more important than any other decision, because it determines all others and influences all others. If I think of myself as a victim, I will behave as a victim and come across as a victim. If I think of myself as less than, I will behave in ways that are less than and I will appear that way to others. If I judge others, I will behave in ways that offend them and thus keep love at bay.

Yet all these deadly games begin to grow old after a while, not only to us but to those around us. I can think of few more cringe-filled experiences than looking around and realizing that people find you pathetic—or worse.

This might be the moment when you realize that your way isn't working. When you grow sick and tired of being sick and tired. That's often when people fall to their knees, looking for an escape from their habitual patterns of self-sabotage and pain.

Such a moment, of course, is not a eureka experience that automatically changes everything. Simply knowing that we need to change doesn't necessarily mean we know how to. Often our emotional muscles have congealed around mental habits that formed so long ago we can't even remember their source. They then burrowed into our subconscious mind and continue to dictate our thoughts and behavior.

When I was growing up, the entrances into many areas of power were still closed to women that are not closed now. It felt as though we had to grow claws on our fingernails in order to make our way into rooms that were much easier for men to enter.

What I found—and I think this is true of many women around my age—is that even when the doors had been opened and I no longer needed my claws, it was as though they'd become cemented into my fingernails. A certain harshness in my personality had become a mental habit, like an emotional muscle that seemed permanently cramped. I imagined opponents who weren't even there, then suffered the consequences of treating people as though they were. For where we don't extend love, we project fear. We are subconsciously setting people up to become who we've already decided they were.

The ego doesn't deny your suffering. It simply says other people are to blame for it—which then maintains the separation, as people keep appearing in your life to constantly disappoint you. What the ego doesn't want you to see are all the subconscious and brilliant ways you set them up to do that.

Spiritual rebirth is not an easy process; like physical birth, it can be messy and difficult. It takes brutal self-honesty to recognize the parts of us that need to die.

First we come to see that a pattern is ego, that it's dysfunctional and doesn't serve us. But that doesn't mean it necessarily goes away, that it immediately stops. If anything, the pattern sometimes seems to become more prevalent, more obvious, as though the Holy Spirit puts a magnifying glass onto that aspect of our personality so we have no choice but to attend to it.

This is why it often feels as though once you get serious about the spiritual path, things can seem to get worse before they get better. Your character defects were operative before, but you were sort of anesthetized to them, able to get by with pretending they weren't much of an issue. But once we do admit we have them, the work begins. You still might behave in a dysfunctional way, but you can no longer pretend to yourself that you're not doing so.

The fact that we're admitting our issues is a good thing, but the ego is very sly here. The ego loves to talk about itself and thoroughly enjoys this part of the process. It doesn't mind you owning your shadow, so long as you blame someone else for why you are the way you are.

Contrary to the psychotherapeutic trend, it doesn't really matter how our neurotic patterns got started. Some say they started with Mommy or Daddy, or with social or ancestral patterns, and all that might be true. But metaphysically it all started millions of years ago with the first thought of separation. All that's happened since then is that we keep repeating it. What matters is not where the fear came from, but that it's lodged in your brain. And analyzing the darkness doesn't necessarily turn on the light.

At a certain point it doesn't really matter where you got your issues. They're yours now. And no matter who your parents were, you can be reparented by God. Your parents birthed your mortal self; God Himself birthed the real you.

We don't heal our lives in the past but in the present. We're not held back by the love we didn't receive in the past but by the love we're refusing to give right now. In this moment, we can make a better choice. But that's not always easy, and sometimes it takes more than simply positive thinking. Sometimes it's not enough to just tell ourselves to act differently. Sometimes we need God's help. And lo and behold, He is always there.

Positively You

The ego is simply a false belief, but beliefs—particularly unrecognized beliefs—are very powerful. The ego is the power of your mind turned against you, in opposition to who you truly are.

The ego will use any scrap of evidence with which to prosecute its case against you: you're too average, too poor, too boring, too uneducated, too unpopular, too young, too old, or whatever else might prove your unworthiness.

If you're skirting failure, it will appear as a fear of failure. It will tell you what a loser you are and make you too afraid to keep trying.

If you're skirting success, it will appear as a fear of success. It will set you up for a fall by telling you that you know more than you actually do.

If you're in a relationship, it will appear as a fear of intimacy. It will tell you it's unsafe to be vulnerable and will create barriers to deep relationship.

If you're not in a relationship, it will make you cynical. It will tell you that you'll never find someone and there aren't any good people out there anyway.

The ego will use anything—from your past or your present—to convince you that the world is a dangerous place and that everyone, including you, just isn't good enough.

Thinking such things, we shrivel. We become defensive rather than openhearted, critical rather than forgiving, always seeing a reason to blame rather than bless, inventing sometimes the cleverest ways to cast others from our heart.

The anxiety and depression that result from all this don't mean that something is wrong with you. This is soul pain. Soul pain is a functional response to living a life so deeply at odds with who we are and why we were born. Just as the brain registers pain if the body is wounded, the psyche registers pain when the soul is wounded. And just as you can't treat bodily pain by simply numbing it, you can't treat psychic pain by simply numbing it either.

For far too many, the human condition is a mental nightmare. And like any nightmare, it feels very real while we're in it. Yet the only way to escape is to awaken. The enlightened masters of the world are called the Awakened Ones for that reason: they've awakened from the illusions that dominate the world.

The purpose of our lives is to heal from the wounds of living in this world, and to help heal others as well. Jesus is in your mind to remind you who you are, to remind you you're more than good enough, to remind you he is with you, and to remind you that miracles are your natural inheritance.

You are no better and no worse than anyone else. All the children of God are special, and none of the children of God is special* (T-12; T-313). You are as God created you. Remembering this is liberation from all manner of psychic pain.

Your mistakes have no power to uncreate what God created. The ego is both that which sets us up to do the wrong thing and that which punishes us savagely for having done so. God is not that which sends us to hell, but that which delivers us from it. He desires to correct our mistakes, not punish us for them. The Atonement is an expression of God's infinite mercy, a way to realign with our innocence no matter how far we have strayed from it.

Another way to live means another way to be. Another way to be means another way to think. Another way to think becomes a different way to act. And a different way of acting then creates a different life.

One of my favorite quotes is said to be from author George Eliot: "It is never too late to be what you might have been." I remember how that sentence struck me when I first saw it, and it still feels so true to me every time I read it.

We can give birth to a better version of ourselves. We are healed of the wounds that belong to a self with which we no longer identify.

Again, is this denial? Yes. It is *positive* denial. It is denying the effects of a lie and affirming the power of a no longer deniable truth.

Who you are is an unalterable, eternal creation of God. Your true self is an undeletable file. The fact that it's unchosen doesn't mean it's been deleted from the computer.

Something in you *does* know how to live life successfully; you're programmed by God to do so. But the problem is that your inner computer got hacked. Learned powerlessness is a common ploy of the ego mind, convincing you you're fundamentally broken in order to ensure that you always will be. The voice that tells you that you cannot change is not the voice of love. Allow the voice of Jesus to drown it out.

As with everything else, practice does make perfect.

There's no more important effort in life than becoming who we are capable of being. Yet the ego loves to ingratiate itself into the process. It gives us endless excuses for bad behavior while we're "working on ourselves." Yes, we need to own our shadow, but we also need to own our light. In the separation lies your weakness, and in your oneness with God lies your strength. Jesus is a way of remembering that such strength is there.

Spirit is the loving use of your mind; salvation therefore is a psychological process. The fundamental shift is from a constant and almost pathological obsession with analyzing the darkness, to a creative and proactive determination to receive, to own, and to embody the light. Remembering Jesus, you remember who you're capable of being.

I remember years ago a woman at one of my lectures asking me what to do to get past a pattern she had of acting like a scolding mother toward her husband. The audience looked eagerly in my direction to see whether I had some insight that might help her unravel this dysfunctional behavioral pattern.

My response was based on years of experience with myself and others.

"Yes, I do," I said slowly. "Don't do it anymore."

She got it. I saw it from the look on her face. And the room did too. There's more power in practicing being who we want to be than in constantly analyzing why we're not already. The ego simply doesn't want us to realize we can choose another way.

There's no more powerful prayer than this: "Dear God, I know I act this way, but I am willing not to. I am willing to change. Please show me how. Amen."

It doesn't mean that from this day forward we're going to be all better, problem handled, personality changed. But it does mean we're on our way; we've begun the process of fundamental change.

Facing our defects is one of the ways we address our wounds, not by blaming others but by holding ourselves accountable. And as we do, the universe supports us. In the places where we got it wrong before, we're even better once we learn to do things right. For we have become humbler. We've been taken down a notch, perhaps, but sometimes that isn't bad news—it's good news.

Years ago, I knew a woman who was quite a character, fun and relatable but also grandiose and boisterous and over the top. She was entertaining for sure, but most people would have put her in the category of a bit too much.

A couple of years after I met her, I was watching a popular new comedy show on television. It featured a character who must have been based on her. Same town, same profession, same manner-isms. Hilarious, yes, but at the same time I thought to myself how humiliating this would have to be for her. Literally millions of people were now laughing at her as much as with her.

When I saw her again about a year later, she had clearly changed. There was a calm and a humility and even an elegance to her that I would never have expected. I didn't want to embar-rass her by bringing up the show, but I did say something about how she seemed quite different.

She looked to me as if to say, *Okay, we can cut the bullshit, Marianne.* She simply said, "How could I not have? It was that, or I would have died."

Good for her. She went through a fire and came out more beau-tiful on the other side. She learned through pain, but she learned.

More Powerful than All the Powers of the World

There really is no world outside us, since everything we see is a projection of our thoughts. Since all minds are joined, as I heal my own life I am contributing to the healing of the world.

I can't pretend to be part of a global evolutionary change if I'm unwilling to try to change myself. Everything we do is imprinted with the consciousness with which we do it; therefore our thoughts as well as our actions influence the world around us. Pregnancy, whether of a person or of a new civilization, begins with an internal conception, gestates within, and is then brought forth into the world.

The Second Coming is both an individual and collective experience of remembrance, or rebirth. As our relationship to God becomes more real, as we deepen our practice and take spiritual principles more seriously, we begin to attract those whose desires to heal the world are similar to ours. They may or may not share a conscious spiritual perspective, but they are distinguished by their willingness to dedicate their lives to making the world a better place.

It's a law of nature that we attract into our experience that which resonates with our consciousness. The more we uplift our thoughts above the narrow confines of the ego mind, the more we will attract into our experience those whose thoughts are similarly uplifted. And there is a plan to that. The Atonement works not just on the individual level but also collectively. There is not only an individual curriculum for all of us, but also a plan for the salvation of the world that includes the matrix of our relationships. The more you progress spiritually, the more you're joined on your path by "mighty companions"* (MT-11) who, like you, are about their Father's business. That language may or may not mean anything to them, but everyone is on a spiritual path, whether they know it or not. Anyone who is serving love is serving the God of the universe. Not only individuals but relationships are imbued with the potential to become more expansive than the mortal mind can imagine.

Just as the cells of the body are led through a natural intelligence to collaborate with other cells to serve the healthy function of the organ or organism of which they are part, we ourselves are imbued with a natural intelligence leading us to collaborate with others for a greater good. Love *is* the greater good.

As the oak tree is contained within the acorn, your enlightened self is contained within you. As every bud is programmed to become a blossom, you and I are programmed to become the highest actualization of our potential.

Free will, however, means that we can say no to the process. We can obstruct the process of our highest becoming, closing our hearts to God and to each other. The ego is unbelievably sly in its efforts to make sure we do. We are constantly tempted to close our hearts, and by so doing to sabotage our lives.

The Holy Spirit is like spiritual radar, which will always override the dictates of the ego. Yet in the absence of a spiritual practice, we fail to develop the mental habit of listening to and following its guidance. Its signals are always there, but we often don't attend to them. The world is very loud, and the Voice for God is very soft. The ego speaks first, and the ego speaks loudest* (T-100). We learn to quiet the mind so we can hear what God is saying.

Every circumstance, every encounter, every relationship is programmed with divine potential. Every circumstance provides us with the opportunity to be the best that we can be, as well as the challenge not to retreat into ego patterns brought over from the past.

The ego's opposition to following that programming is intense. Since soul connection dissolves the ego, its defenses are ever on guard. The primary weapons in its arsenal are attack thoughts, subtle or overt, toward others or even toward ourselves. We judge more easily than we forgive. The ego doesn't love other people; it exploits other people. As long as our minds do the ego's bidding, we will continue to destroy our relationships, we will continue to suffer, and the world will continue to decline.

God loves all of us as one. Our task is to align our thinking so we can think as God thinks and love as God loves. God's Will means Loving Thought. Every attack thought toward ourselves or others is like a nail in the body of Christ. They are the primary tools by which the ego keeps us stuck within the prison of limited awareness.

From global poverty to war among empires to nuclear bombs, the collective state of humanity is a feast of lovelessness. Our behavioral patterns reflect a deadly state of consciousness, from which we have manifested a dangerous world. Jesus is a name on the door that delivers us to a world beyond that one. It is the same world we see now, transformed by love. It is miraculously saved through a change in our sense of purpose and a change in our sense of ourselves.

The question is how to open the door, how to allow for our escape and seek refuge from the madness that plagues us. The answer is not a broad stroke; it is a willingness on all our parts to see every moment as an opportunity to love. In every such instant, a holy instant, our spiritual birth canal expands by even just a bit as the holy child is brought forth into the world. Upon the birth of Jesus in the manger, as well as upon his rebirth in your heart, the angels sing. The thoughts of Love flow forth to all the world. This child is tiny, innocent, and vulnerable. It might seem like just a tiny thing, a softer and more authentic moment. Yet that child is not your weakness; it's your power—in fact, more powerful than all the powers of the world.

The Small Still Voice Within

Imagine the universe as the pluperfect creation of a divine architect. That creation is a hologram, with each piece of it carrying within it the same perfect architectural plans. Those plans exist for each of us and are available, should we care to download them. Most of us, however, don't even know that they exist.

Our consciousness is like a computer, and these plans exist in an undeletable file. We go about our lives thinking our job is to bring up a blank document and create our own architectural plans. We think we need to create a life for ourselves, when in fact God has already created a path to an ever-greater life for us. He carries in His Mind the image of our perfect life.

God's plan for the salvation of the world involves divine knowing of all beings past, present, and future. Each of us has an equally important part to play in bringing it forth, but the plan itself is beyond the scope of what our mortal minds can yet comprehend. We discover our part by devoting our lives to Him, praying to be the people He would have us be so we can do what He would have us do.

We do much better in life when instead of revealing our plans to God, we ask Him to reveal His plans for us. This is not the abdication of personal responsibility but the assumption of spiritual power. When we stop trying to tell life what it means, life then tells us what it means. Self-will is not self-love, but rather a way of compensating for what we fear is a void in which there is no love or plan for us. In fact, all good emerges from that void, the holy emptiness that only God can fill. God's plan for our salvation will work; ours, so often rooted in fear, will not.

The plan for the healing of the world is much bigger than we are, and as individuals we can't know what part we would best play in carrying it out. The Holy Spirit is like a cosmic central intelligence, knowing exactly how our efforts would be most helpful, where, and in relationship with whom. Learning to listen to the Voice for God, opening our minds and hearts to guidance and illumination that lie beyond the power of logic alone, we become mystics. The mystical path is the path to sustainability in the twenty-first century. It is the partnership of brain and heart, reason and intuition, that is the essence of the enlightened mind. Jesus is a path to achieving it.

Surrender to God means surrender to love, not as a broad stroke but to the best of our ability in any given instant. God's creation is not only perfect; it also responds fully, automatically, and immediately to any mis-creation, or disruption in the field. Like a GPS, it recalculates our path when we have deviated from love. Not only is the universe primed to follow every moment of harmony with another moment of harmony, it is also primed to follow any moment of disharmony with divine correction. The universe is both self-organizing and self-correcting. Perfect love knows how to perfectly repair whatever deviates from perfection.

The world is in a state of deviation from love right now, like a body that is sick. Our purpose on earth is to help heal the world, and every encounter, every effort, either large or small, can be part of that healing.

We are all called to be healers, and God's call goes out to us constantly. It's the call to be better, do better, stop thinking only about ourselves, show up to contribute, forgive, and love. We're assigned by the Holy Spirit to any situation providing maximal opportunity for the healing of the world.

It's up to us, however, whether we choose to take the assignment. The problem is that we often turn down the assignment without realizing it. At no time when I've closed my heart did I wake up that morning intending to be a jerk that day.

The ego's kingdom is the low road of negativity and anger, limitation and fear. It sends us twisting and turning through bad relationships and failed hopes and dreams. But there is a high road, already constructed by the Holy Spirit, which is the path to greater peace and creativity. We don't need to create the high road; we need merely to follow it.

One way or the other, we will be following a path in life. We will either be directed by the cacophonous, angry, fear-based voice of the ego, or by the small still voice within.

The ego is like a malignant cell that has lost connection with its natural intelligence and its collaborative function. The Holy Spirit is our immune system, the medicine, the healing. It is there to direct us, to heal us, but without our conscious cooperation we are often seduced into the ego's madness.

In both Judaism and Christianity there is reference to a "small still voice for God." There is within us a quiet voice that can and will direct us every moment of each day. It is a universal theme that we need to quiet our minds if we wish to hear it. That voice, one expression of which is the mystic Jesus, will speak to us; but it's our responsibility to listen.

Many times people have said to me, "I don't know what God is telling me," and I've responded based on my own experience: "Oh, yes, you do. You just don't *like* what God is telling you." We think we know better. We get an intuitive hit, or a sense we've received an answer when we pray about something, but it might seem to make no logical sense. After all, the Holy Spirit knows what's going to happen tomorrow, and we don't. So we say, "I'll ask Him again tomorrow, when He has more data."

When we make the quieting of our minds a fundamental lifestyle decision, we do begin to experience love's intuitive presence. Its voice was always there; we just didn't know to take it seriously. Many times in my past, I absolutely had the sense of an answer to my prayer for guidance; yet because it went against "expert opinions," I ignored it, only later to realize what a mistake I had made. Other times, I simply didn't take the time to ask, to pray, to deeply reflect on a question, only later to realize my lack of wisdom. Yet the voice was always there.

The Voice for God is that which guides us toward love, forgiveness, right living, and faith. It's a part of our mind that can see the whole picture in a way we can't, that knows what's going to happen tomorrow and how our part best fits into a larger plan.

"He speaks from nearer than your heart to you. His Voice is closer than your hand"* (WB-226).

As it says in the *Course*, all of us live with a consistent stream of thoughts in the background of our minds. Such thoughts fit basically into one of two categories: either a cacophonous background noise filled with fear-based perceptions, or a peaceful symphony of positivity and love. Prayer and meditation dissolve the former and increase the latter.

Thoughts of random negativity emerge fully formed from the cave of the ego mind. They are the inevitable results of a fear-based view of the world. They arise from fear, and they perpetuate fear. Efforts to suppress them only make them more dangerous. Telling yourself to "stop thinking like that" is a losing battle, because you're simply pitting you against you.

The Voice for God is the exact opposite of the voice of the ego. It is the voice that reminds us we were created innocent, and so we are. It reminds us our mistakes do not eradicate our innocence, that we can atone for them and we can change. It reminds us that this is also true of everyone else; that people make mistakes, yes, but we can extend our perception beyond their errors to see the truth of who they are. It is the voice reminding us we can always be more gentle, less judgmental, kinder, less arrogant, less negative, more responsible, more ethical, and less quick to blame others for faults of our own. It reminds us that those kinds of qualities, being expressions of love, are magnets for miracles.

Listening to the Voice for God is a habit we cultivate, the mental musculature of grace. Who among us hasn't decided something we came later to regret, remembering that at the time we'd had a gut feeling it just wasn't right? But we'd gone with some worldly voice that said differently, allowing it to override our internal knowing. Walking through life taking seriously the guidance of the Holy Spirit, the mystic Jesus, the Voice for God, we know that the voices of the world should always be listened to, but they should never ever have the final say.

Prayer

The highest level of prayer is not an entreaty of any kind. It's a gentle communion with that which is bigger than ourselves. Our communion with God is the ultimate experience of ourselves. God speaks to us, and in prayer we speak to Him.

Prayer is the way we invoke and activate the power of God in our lives, drawing down the intercessionary power of love to change our lives by changing us.

Sometimes someone will tell me they have a problem in their life, and I'll ask if they've prayed about it.

I'll often get the answer, "Oh, I know it's in God's hands."

"But that's not what I asked you," I'll say. "I asked if you prayed about it."

For the two are very different things. To know something is in God's hands is very different from actually putting it there. To know something is in God's hands means you know that ultimately love will prevail. To actually *put* something in God's hands means that of your own free will you're putting yourself in service to the goal. At the very least, that will speed things up.

Putting something in the hands of God means we're willing to think about it differently. No matter what has happened, it's the space we inhabit within an experience—the thoughts and behavior with which we respond to it—that will ultimately determine its effect.

The highest level of prayer is for another way to think about something. Thought is the level of cause, and the direct relationship between cause and effect is inviolable. Jesus works with us on the causal level. He cannot and will not take away the effects of our thinking, but if we ask him to, he will help us change our thoughts. The choice for love is a choice for peace, for healing, and for miracles. For miracles are natural wherever there is love.

We can't say, "Dear God, I'm holding on to my negativity, but please change the effects that all those negative thoughts have caused in my life, okay?"

Not gonna happen.

What we *can* do, however, is to pray that God take away our negativity. Putting a relationship in the hands of God, for instance, means asking for help in seeing someone else's innocence and in showing ours to them. Even one person—"whoever is saner at the time"* (T-384)—can change the trajectory of a conflicted relationship. The prayer is that our thoughts be shifted from a focus on blame to a focus on innocence.

We can pray:

> *Dear God,*
> *I am willing not to be cold,*
> *I am willing not to be harsh,*
> *I am willing not to be judgmental.*
> *Please enter the deepest regions of my mind,*
> *show me my errors, and change my thoughts.*

Free me from my self-sabotaging ways.
Change me in my deepest heart
that I might have a miracle.
Amen

Jesus cannot do our work *for* us, but he will do our work with us. He will not and cannot take away the effects of our thinking, but he is always there to help us think more wisely.

Prayer is a tool in our toolbox too often set aside in favor of far lesser powers. I find it amusing when people say, "All we can do now is pray," as though all the really powerful things have already been tried.

It's often said that there are no atheists in foxholes, but we don't have to wait until a crisis arrives to create a better life for ourselves. You come to the point where you don't just pray when things are going poorly; you pray so they'll go well. Prayer is like preventive medicine for the soul. We are responsible for how we direct our thoughts, and as we direct our mind to embrace the light, darkness has a much harder time getting in. Mental energy that is consciously placed in the service of love is unavailable to the ego's purposes.

The Lord's Prayer is an example of a powerful invocation for a miracle-minded existence.

Our Father—*Our true source*

Who art in heaven—*In the awareness of our oneness*

Hallowed be thy name—*May the meaningless stimulus of*
  the world fall away that I might realize the sacred

Thy kingdom come—*May the energies of love prevail*

Thy Will be done—*May loving thought, not ego, be manifest*

On earth as it is in heaven—*Not just abstractly on the level*
  of thought, but in my practical experience

Give us this day our daily bread—*May our minds be open to receive the infinite abundance of life*

And forgive us our trespasses—*Correct our thinking, return us to the state of our innocence*

As we forgive those who trespass against us—*Help us see the innocence in others, that we might see it in ourselves*

Leave us not in temptation—*Guard our minds so we won't wander into thoughts of ego and fear*

But deliver us from evil—*Guide us away from sick and loveless thoughts*

For Thine is the kingdom, and Thine is the power, and Thine is the glory—*Love is the kingdom, love is the power, love is the glory*

Forever and ever—*Every moment of the day*

Amen—*May it be so*

"The world you see must be denied, for sight of it is costing you a different kind of vision. You cannot see both worlds, for each of them involves a different kind of seeing, and depends on what you cherish"* (T-254). Looking at the world through the eyes of love, we do not see fear. But looking at the world through the eyes of fear, we cannot see love.

By acknowledging that God's kingdom is the kingdom with which we choose to identify, we are empowering ourselves. We are determining which universe we choose to inhabit. When we choose love, fear cannot choose us.

Prayer is a mighty power. But not only does the ego resist praying; it also resists giving God any credit when the prayer works! It's remarkable how many times I've seen people express despair and hopelessness about a situation, have it change dramatically after they've prayed about it, then react almost casually when things turn around for the better.

God certainly doesn't care; He has no ego with which to be offended by our lack of acknowledgment. But saying "Thank you, God" is a far more powerful use of the mind than saying "Yeah, it turned out better than I expected after all." It's a way of reminding your mind of all the power that it holds.

Your Holiness

Our vulnerability and mildness are spiritual strengths, although the ego views them as weaknesses. The three kings bowed before the Christ child; the Christ child didn't bow before them. There is no power in the world that's greater than the power of love.

The mystic Jesus is a reminder of this. His name is a signal to the subconscious mind that you are more than the world has told you that you are. To say you were made in the image of God means you are an idea in His mind, and ideas do not leave their source. Your bond is inseparable. Every problem we have in life stems from just that fact: we have forgotten who we are. Forgetting who we are, we forget where we came from. Forgetting who we are, we forget we are one with each other. Forgetting who we are, we forget why we are here.

Jesus helps us remember. In remembering who we are, we remember that our love, not our fear, is our true identity. Our love is not our weakness; it is the strength of God within us. A more compassionate, more regenerative, more nurturing consciousness is in fact the only way to a survivable future for the human race.

The Christ is a facet of your psyche, the melding of your heart and mind. It is holy because it is whole. There is no power that can stand against it. There is nothing your holiness cannot do.

This section from *A Course in Miracles* describes the power of our holiness:

> *Your holiness reverses all the laws of the world. It*
> *is beyond every restriction of time, space, distance,*
> *and limits of any kind. Your holiness is totally*
> *unlimited in its power because it establishes you as a*
> *Son of God, at one with the Mind of his Creator.*
>
> *Through your holiness the power of God is made manifest.*
> *Through your holiness the power of God is made available.*
> *And there is nothing the power of God cannot do. Your*
> *holiness, then, can remove all pain, can end all sorrow,*
> *and can solve all problems. It can do so in connection with*
> *yourself and with anyone else. It is equal in its power to help*
> *anyone because it is equal in its power to save anyone.*
>
> *If you are holy, so is everything God created. You*
> *are holy because all things He created are holy. And all*
> *things He created are holy because you are.* * (WB-58)*

The thinking of God is 180 degrees away from the thinking of the world. One of the places where our thinking is particularly upside-down is regarding arrogance and humility. It isn't arrogant to say the power of God is within you; what would be arrogant is to think it's not. Wouldn't that mean you were a creation of something other than Him? You are powerful because of a power that is in you, but not *of* you. To claim that power, and seek to use it well, is not arrogant but humble.

The mystic Jesus puts our perceptions in right alignment.

Surrendering our thoughts to him, our perceptions are illuminated, lifted above the limitations of our routine thought patterns. If we identify with our weakness, the vicissitudes of weakness will be the reality we experience. If we identify with Christ, we will be lifted to a higher realization that (1) love is who we are, (2) miracles occur naturally as expressions of love, and (3) we were not created to be at the effect of lovelessness in ourselves or in others. Disciplining our minds to remember those things, whatever our spiritual practice, is the assumption of the power of Christ.

As your thoughts are lifted above the illusions of the world, you automatically help lift others—for all minds are joined. Thinking with love, we don't simply experience miracles for ourselves. We become miracle workers in the lives of others. It's not only our own lives that we are here to heal; in healing ourselves we help to heal the world.

The real you is not at the effect of limitations imposed by the ego mind. Which world you identify with is your choice. If you identify only with the mortal world, then the mortal world has power over you. If you identify with the spiritual world, you have power to transform the mortal. Identifying with our separate needs, separate desires, and separate self, we are limited to the laws that prevail within the ego's domain. But identifying with our holiness, we are under no laws but God's* (WB-134).

None of this means, of course, that I can walk off the roof of a high-rise building and not fall to the ground. It does mean, however, that I need not be bound by the shackles of false beliefs. The universe of God is literally limitless. To the extent that I align my thinking with the thoughts of God, so am I.

We are born into this world as physical beings, but spiritually we can be twice born. We can choose to be reparented by God and receive the unlimited spiritual riches that are our natural inheritance.

Spiritual maturity is an aspect of personal maturity. There doesn't come a day when you "get there"; you just evolve over time into a more sophisticated person. Miracle-mindedness simply becomes the rule rather than the exception in how we live our lives. As it is written in *A Course in Miracles*, "miracles are everyone's right, but purification is necessary first"* (T-3). We must purify the mind of darkness before we can see the light. Only when our minds are purified of judgment, attack, self-reference, and unforgiveness can we experience the miracle of a life that works.

We can see every situation as an opportunity to purify ourselves of the mental plaque that has accumulated since yesterday. We can say about any circumstance, "The last time something like this happened, how did I play it? Was I openhearted, or closed? Kind or uncaring? How can I do better now? Which aspect of myself do I choose to express? My wounded self, or my holy self?" Every situation is both an invitation to express our holiness and a temptation to display our wound.

Remembering the mystic Jesus, I remember who I am. And as I remember that I am not my wounds, my wounds begin to heal.

Cinderella

Everything in life is a projection of what we've already decided to see. We see in life what we expect to see. Expecting to see miracles is simply a change in focus, from thoughts of limitation to thoughts of infinite possibility.

Waking up each morning and casting your love before you is the most powerful way to plan your day. It directs the subconscious mind to notice those things that are good and generative, consciously disregarding elements of fear that are always lurking on the periphery of our minds.

The words "disciple" and "discipline" come from the same root, after all. Enlightenment is a mind training, in which we consciously take responsibility for the nature of our thoughts. We needn't surrender our thoughts to fear; instead, we can surrender them to love. The discipline of spiritual practice is everything. If you don't turn on the light in a room, it's ridiculous to curse the darkness.

Turning on that light—dedicating ourselves to love—we begin to discern patterns of goodness and opportunity that are otherwise obscured. We come to see how much good is always available to us. Everything we need is either right in front of us or is on the way, because that's how God's universe operates. Living with that realization is a powerful rearrangement of our assumptions, expectations, and mental filters.

Sometimes we miss out on a miracle for the simple reason that it seemed too easy. We can't imagine that the universe could be designed so perfectly that whatever will support our growth is always right in front of us. But it is. We're trained to think in a very limited way; therefore limits are pretty much all we see.

In my past, there were two gigantic professional opportunities that I turned down. I realize that the reason I turned them down was because I failed to recognize their importance at the time. The fact that they both just landed in front of me like feathers falling into my lap made me underestimate their importance. I couldn't imagine that something that easy could be that important. To the ego, struggle is the generator of significance. To the spirit, effortless accomplishment is simply a by-product of right living. It took me a while to notice that flowers don't struggle to blossom.

I had been taught by the world not to expect miracles; therefore I didn't see them even though they were right in front of me. I had not yet realized that "out of the blue" means out of the field of quantum possibility.

Once when my daughter was a little girl, we were watching a video of *Cinderella*. In the scene where the wicked stepmother (the ego) and her awful daughters (the committee of ugly thoughts in your head that tell you how awful you are all the time) have left Cinderella (your innocence) behind to go to the ball, Cinderella falls to the ground weeping.

Then the Fairy Godmother (the Holy Spirit) appears! So guess what happens then? In the video we were watching, Cinderella said to the Fairy Godmother, "Oh, Fairy Godmother, I thought you'd never get here!"—and the Fairy Godmother responded, "Oh that's not true, dear, or I couldn't have come!!"

Read that one again.

So if Cinderella hadn't considered the possibility that she existed, the Fairy Godmother would still have been there, *but Cinderella would not have seen her.* We must at least be *open* to the possibility of infinite possibility, or no matter how many miracles occur the ego will be successful at nullifying their existence. That's why faith means faith in that which is yet unseen.

Given that Cinderella had no dress to wear, no carriage to take her, and no horses to draw the carriage, there was obviously no way that girl was going to the ball.

The Fairy Godmother could not have arrived had Cinderella been a different kind of girl. In order for the mean-spirited will of the wicked stepmother to be countermanded—in order for another way to be paved by which Cinderella could get to the ball—it was necessary for Cinderella's consciousness to be receptive to miracles. If she had starting screaming about her stepmother and stepsisters, "I *hate* those f—— bitches!" then the Fairy Godmother could not have come. Her appearance was predicated on two things: (1) Cinderella's faith that it was possible, and (2) Cinderella's innocent heart, which allowed her to feel her grief but not project it outward as an attack on those she perceived as having caused it.

Continuing with the story, it's instructive to see what happened next.

The Fairy Godmother, like Merlin and other magicians, has a wand just as Moses had a rod. The wand and rod symbolize straight and disciplined mental adherence to spiritual truth. They symbolize the conviction from which miracles arise.

The Fairy Godmother didn't call for an Uber to take Cinderella to the ball, nor did she call Neiman Marcus for the perfect dress.

She didn't change Cinderella's circumstances; she transformed the ones that already existed. Her wand touched a pumpkin and surrounded it with light; that turned it into a coach. Her wand touched the mice and surrounded them with light; that turned them into coachmen. She touched Cinderella's rags and surrounded them with light; that turned them into a ball gown. The Fairy Godmother is that which reinterprets everything, and everything miraculously transforms. Throwing her wand in the direction of something, she simply "saw it in a new light."

The Fairy Godmother retreats into the ethers when unneeded. But the ethers are within your mind and when you need her, she is there.

Cinderella is who you really are, and when you're clear about that, the wicked stepmother loses her power over you. She can keep that stupid house she lives in; it's not your real home anyway. You're moving into the castle with the prince, and you know who *that* is.

The world as we know it will teach our children things they're going to have to spend years learning how to forget. Fairy tales are preparatory learning of a different kind. They are a way to both teach our children and help them retain an understanding of the miraculous world. A pumpkin turns into a coach, then water turns into wine, then loaves and fishes multiply.

It's all the same thing.

The Meaning of Now

Time is a learning device. It's a screen onto which we see our thoughts projected. It's actually an illusion of consciousness, real within the three-dimensional world but not within the ultimate reality of spirit. In the words of Albert Einstein, "Time and space are illusions of consciousness, albeit persistent ones."

While there are three categories of time—past, present, and future—only one is ever really happening at all. Past and future exist only in the mind. The only place where God's time—that is, eternity—intersects linear time is in the present.

The present moment is our point of power. It is the link with eternal reality, from which new beginnings are always possible. That is the miracle, and the meaning, and the power of now.

A present moment untarnished by loveless memories from the past is called in the *Course* the Holy Instant. We are born again in any moment when we don't bring the past with us. The reason the image of the Christ is a newborn child is because he has no past.

A traditional model of psychotherapy is obsessed with exploring the past. A spiritual model of psychotherapy sees no point in doing so. For the past exists only in our minds, and in a very real way didn't even happen the way we think it did. The brain picks and chooses from a myriad of memories the way the eye picks and chooses from a myriad of visual stimuli.

The ego's propensity for obsession with both past and future is a characteristically sly way of obstructing our vision. The most powerful thing we can do with the past is to put it in the hands of God. The role of the Holy Spirit, the gift of the mystic Jesus, is that he will change our mind about it for us. Is looking at the past a part of our healing? Sometimes, yes. But only so we can atone for our mistakes and forgive others for theirs.

The ego is like a set of blinders: looking at guilt, focusing on past or future, it shields us from a vision of the miraculous. We do it all the time. Constantly looking at the past, dwelling on where we or others got it wrong, is not the way to heal. We don't get rid of darkness by hitting it with a baseball bat, but by turning on the light. We don't spiritually transform by destroying our demons; we transform by giving birth to the angel that we are. In the presence of light, darkness disappears. This isn't a spiritual bypass; it's spiritual alchemy.

The Holy Spirit dwells in a realm of timelessness but operates in time. He is that which mediates between your spiritual and your material selves, building a bridge between the two. He sees who you really are, and He also sees who you are within the world. It is His job to help the two become one, as they are in Jesus.

Jesus is the mind in which only love is real. All that was real in the past was the love you gave and the love you received; everything else was mere illusion of consciousness. There is no need to bring anything into the present from the past except that love. All else is our proverbial "baggage."

In giving your past to Jesus, you're asking that he change your mind about it for you. You're asking that he dissolve any memories that make lovelessness real in your perceptions to-day, thus freeing you from their effects. In forgiving both your-self and others from the sins—that is, mistakes—of the past, you are free to begin again. The universe is always ready to start over when you are.

If my mind is obsessed with the past while in the present, I block future opportunities. They're there, but I won't see them. Dragging the past into the present, we bring shadow figures that cloud our eyes, obstructing the arrival of relationships and cir-cumstances that could create a new beginning.

Bringing the past into the present, I'm programming the future to be just like the past. Then the ego gets to say, "See, I told you. Nothing ever changes."

The Holy Instant interrupts linear time, giving us in any mo-ment the miraculous opportunity for new beginnings. It is a kind of cosmic reset in which any effects from the past except love are nullified, since only love exists. In that moment, releasing our at-tachment to the past and surrendering the future into the hands of God, we heal both. In an instant we can release all thoughts ex-cept love. That's how the universe corrects itself, but only if we're aligned with that intention. The present can't free us if we're insis-tent on living in the past.

When I was a child my sister and I had what were called "add-a-pearl" necklaces. Every holiday we would receive another little pearl to put on a chain, the idea being that one day we would have a full necklace. I don't remember that either one of us ever did, but I've always thought of the Holy Instant—that moment when all obsession with past and future and guilt and shame have fallen away—as a pearl we're adding to a collection of perfect moments. It's the idea that you could collect these miraculous moments, which might then turn into a minute, which might then turn into an hour, which might then turn into a day, and ultimately transform your life. "Happily ever after" means a state of mind in which we live fully in the present moment, our minds untarnished either by painful memories from the past or obsession about the future.

One of my personal challenges is that sometimes I have difficulty letting the past go. I'll obsess about something that happened in the past rather than allowing for a miracle in the present. "But you said ... !" "But then why did you do that ... ?" The past never has a chance to heal if we ourselves insist on dwelling there. The only thing real about the past was the love we were given and the love we received; the present is programmed to correct all lovelessness that occurred there, as long as we are willing to let it go.

In the Holy Instant we are radically open to the only thing that's real, casting out what isn't real and allowing the universe to begin again. But we can't be open to "the universe" unless we are willing to be open to people. We cannot forgive someone, yet at the same time hold them to their past. Whether it's reminding ourselves of what we did wrong in the past, or reminding others of how they did us wrong in the past, at a certain point even going there is just a way of reopening the wound.

Obviously, at times we need to process things from the past; but there's a difference between processing and spewing. There is a difference between honoring our pain and indulging it. Spirit might need to process, but the ego wants to hold on too long. There's a discipline to knowing when enough has been said.

Of course we shouldn't ignore our suffering. We should always honor the season of our pain. But the ego tempts us to stay on the cross longer than we need to at times, which is just as dysfunctional as ignoring our suffering altogether. The ego would turn past pain into our personal calling card, a sly trick of the ego to keep us mired in its suffering. Learn from it, grow from it, forgive it, and use it to help others. But if I overidentify with the pain in my past, I cannot transcend it. What I haven't yet transcended, I can't help you transcend either. The ultimate question regarding past pain is this: How have the lessons I learned from that experience made me a wiser and better person now?

In the Holy Instant we have a chance to both heal the past and reprogram the future. Jesus is the right alignment of past and future because his mind is the right alignment of everything. We place our past in his hands so he can help us reinterpret it. A past that is forgiven is a past that can no longer touch you, and a future surrendered into the hands of God is a future that will be aligned with divine intelligence.

The Holy Spirit delivers us beyond the limitations of linear time to a realization of timelessness. He keeps us focused on the present because that is the only time that ultimately exists. In Him, both past and future dissolve in the blinding light of what really is, right now. The past is purified of painful memories that do not serve, and the future is programmed to be its most wonderful best.

The most powerful way to plan the future is not by obsessing about it, but by living fully in the present. Miracles occur naturally when we allow them to. The ego doesn't want us to experience the fullness of the present because that's where miracles happen. The ego wants us constantly obsessing about past or future so that our lives will never truly move forward but remain stuck on a never-ending wheel of chronic anxiety and pain.

Only the enlightened master has made every moment a Holy Instant, but all of us, with practice, can build the musculature of the Holy Instant. Only love is real, only the present is real, and nothing else exists. It's amazing how many sentences you delete before pushing the "send" button, once you realize how many things really don't need to be said again.

Miracles collapse time* (T-8), which means we can make a loving decision in any moment, saving time and jumping ahead to a peaceful outcome in any situation. "Only infinite patience produces immediate effects* (T-88). Or we can fill the present with attack or defense, over and over for however long it takes, experiencing the pain of having chosen wrongly as many times as we choose until we are willing to choose again. We can choose fear and drag this thing out, or choose love and make an immediate ascent.

Dear God,
Please save me
from the endless torment of attachment
to past or future.
Send Your spirit to heal my mind
of the temptation to enter
the nothingness of time.
Keep me firmly in the present
that I might know that I am blessed.
Amen

CHAPTER THREE

THE TEMPLES OF RELATIONSHIP

My holy brother, I would enter into all your relationships and step between you and your fantasies. Let my relationship to you be real to you, and let me bring reality to your perception of your brothers. They were not created to enable you to hurt yourself through them. They were created to create with you. This is the truth that I would interpose between you and your goal of madness. Be not separate from me, and let not the holy purpose of Atonement be lost to you in dreams of vengeance. Relationships in which such dreams are cherished have excluded me. Let me enter in the Name of God and bring you peace, that you may offer peace to me.* (T-357)

DRIVING UP TO a fashionable spiritual center, I saw a large sign near the entrance. It said, "Love Yourself."

That's become a trendy thing to say these days, but I thought about what Jesus would have said. He didn't say, "Love yourself." He said, "Love one another."

Not that loving ourselves is bad. It's both the foundation and the result of our ability to love others. Judging ourselves is no less blasphemous than judging others.

But the current glorification of self—the "love yourself" culture—has helped create an atomized society of isolated beings, struggling to relate to one another and grieving the loss of love. Looking in the mirror to say "I love you" all the time doesn't quite cut it long term. It's not even that we're looking for love in all the wrong places. It's that we're not really looking for love at all.

We're looking for sales, we're looking for clicks, we're looking for prestige, we're looking for power, we're looking for things, we're looking to hook up. But that's not the same as looking for love. Perhaps we've even given up on that.

Love is hard to find out there because it isn't out there. It's in here. On the material plane, what we give away we no longer have. On the spiritual plane, we only get to keep what we give away. The only way to find love is to give it.

Too many times a therapist will say, "Why do you think you always pick the same man?" when perhaps it would serve the client best if the therapist asked, "Why do you think you always act a certain way with men?" In other words, why do you push love away? You seem to pick the same man because you keep acting the same way.

In many cases, contemporary psychotherapy has become a cult of blaming someone else. Often it's the ego's hotbed of grievances and victimization, using modern buzzwords like "trauma" and "narcissist" to pretty much explain everything. While those words are meaningful and carry significant messages given by important voices in the culture, they shouldn't be cookie-cutter solutions applied to every single issue. They've been cheapened so much at this point that they're used as a description, an excuse, an almost jingoistic label slapped onto every problem. And notice how rarely the problem seems to be you.

While your therapist is explaining that the person you dated was probably a narcissist, consider whether that person might be talking to their therapist on the other side of town and hearing that you are! The ego just loves to talk about other people's issues, and brilliantly ignores our own.

I spent years in and out of therapy, and often with smart and very wise people. But I think I would have been better served if I'd been coddled much less and busted much more. Therapy should not be a place where we are bolstered in our belief that we're weak, or victimized, or forever harmed. It should be a place where we are aided in letting go of the barriers that stand in front of our hearts, that the love that is all around us might enter in and give us peace.

"Your task is not to seek for love, but merely to seek and find all of the barriers within yourself that you have built against it"* (T-338). Most of us, if we're honest with ourselves, could write down on a piece of paper some of the things we do that drive other people crazy. And if we don't know what those things are, our best friends could probably tell us.

It's our own behavioral patterns more than anything else that deprive us of love. We continue to grasp for love, when usually what we most need to do is identify the ways we push it away. Our souls are swimming every moment in an ocean of love, for that is God's universe. But the ego is truly a sly opponent, being, after all, our own mind turned against us. The biggest mistakes I've made in love I actually thought were a good idea at the time.

Send love to your friends, to your family, to your customers, to your clients, to your boss, to your colleagues, to your employees, to the people you know, to the people you don't know, to your president, and yes—to that ex-president too. Send love to Nancy Pelosi and to Marjorie Taylor Greene. Jesus would. Martin Luther King Jr. said, "God said I have to love my enemies; He didn't say I have to like them."

The world we're living in today is saturated by a mental poison. It is more than toxic; it's hateful. And all of us know it. None of us can afford to sit out the process of doing what we can to de-escalate the madness.

And it has to start with us. With every thought we think we're either adding to the solution or adding to the problem. Either our heart is opened or our heart is closed. There is a way to disagree, to set boundaries, even to oppose behavior that is intolerable, without withholding love. That is the message of Jesus. It is as radical today as it was two thousand years ago.

While I was writing this book, focusing deeply and sincerely on what it would mean to truly deeply love, my assistant made an administrative mistake, and I made a snarky comment. Sometimes people have the extraordinary audacity not to do exactly what we want them to do. Shocking, but it happens.

That's what makes a relationship the ultimate teaching and learning opportunity. The point is not that other people have to change, but that we do. The work is always on ourselves. The ego is certain that a relationship will be fine as soon as the other person starts acting differently. But the fact that we can't accept them as they are acting *now* is the actual problem.

What a victim I was! Couldn't she see that I was trying to write a book and I needed support here, dammit?!?

There was a time in my life when I would have seen the situation that way—as simply about me not attracting the support I needed. But this wasn't some random event ironically at odds with the book that I was writing. It was an exact *reflection* of the book I was writing. The fact that I'm writing about these things brought up all the ways in which I'm not yet living them. That is how perfectly the cosmic computer works.

If my only response to an assistant who doesn't do as I wish is simply to get angry, then I'm limiting my ability to find the words or behavior that can help her do better. It also keeps me from having larger clarity about the relationship as a whole. This isn't about her. It's about me.

But what about healthy boundaries? When is it okay to hold someone else accountable? I threw such questions at Jesus as I made a cup of coffee and slammed shut a cabinet door. "Yeah, I'm sorry you're going through this" was all I could imagine him saying at the time.

I know it's okay to set healthy boundaries, disagree when necessary, and hold someone else accountable. But all those things can and must be done with respect and love. When we attack another person, we're wrong even if we're right. The issues we're here to monitor are our own.

My ego would argue that the problem was her behavior; the Spirit points out that the problem is my anger. Situations such as that will continue as long as I consistently push up against the same wall. But the wall isn't going to give; I have to. That wall is the place—and most of us have one—at which point we can't see how to act with love and still get our needs met. But we're going to have to learn. The situation is going to repeat itself until we do.

So what do we do in such situations? Pray for a miracle. Pray for a shift in perception. Say you're willing to see the situation differently.

Sit down, breathe, pray, and your perceptions will begin to shift. As your mind begins to calm down, one of two things will happen:

1. Your guidance will be to say nothing, to absorb the moment and just let it pass.

OR

2. Your guidance will be that something does need to be said, but you'll be given the wisdom to say what you need to say at just the right time and in just the right way. You'll be guided not only in what you should say but in who to be while you're saying it. The Holy Spirit doesn't handle situations for you, but turns you into a person who knows how to handle them yourself.

The main point is to see that the problem is within yourself; therefore so is the solution. If you think the only solution is to find someone else to fulfill whatever function you had assigned to that person, you'll simply attract someone else who acts the same way, or whom you subconsciously set up to act the same way, until your eyes are opened to the real issue: *you!*

The universe is intentional. It is always nudging us to be better, and if that means putting people in our lives who make us have to confront our own barriers to love, then it will.

"This is my commandment, that ye love one another, even as I have loved you" (John 15:12, ASV).

To say this is easy; to live it is hard. That's why the mystic Jesus is so relevant and important. Whether through religion or psychotherapy, the world is in desperate need today of lessons in how to love.

Both are the healing of the mind. Religion is limited when it lacks psychological astuteness, and psychotherapy is limited when it lacks spiritual understanding. There are voices within both these days transforming them into genuinely spiritual pursuits. Whether in psychotherapy or at a religious service, the greatest gift we can receive is a reminder to give more love.

The ego loves to use both religion and psychotherapy for its purposes, and clearly that includes the Christian religion as much as any other. But there's no legitimate conversation about Jesus that's not a conversation about love. Reclaiming the radicalism of love is the only way of claiming a radical relationship with Jesus, and the radical love of Jesus is the true nature of the self.

Relationship to God

Every circumstance involves a relationship: our relationship to God, our relationship to ourselves, our relationship to other people, or our relationship to the world.

Some would say we have no relationship to God because there is no God. There are just atoms and particles that make up an amazing but ultimately meaningless goop. That means we're floating in a random universe where whatever meaning life has for us is the meaning we bring to it. That's a respectable existential argument, but it's a lonely one. It leaves us very much on our own. It posits no "cosmic companionship," as Martin Luther King Jr. referred to the Holy Spirit's presence in our lives. If you believe you're on your own, *in your experience then you will be*. This gives no sense of comfort, denying ourselves our inheritance of either power or love.

Then there are those who do believe in God but see Him as a judgmental long-bearded man in the sky, just waiting for us to screw up and not do what He told us to do so He can send us to the depths of hell. Such a God is a God made in man's image rather than the other way around. The notion of an angry God is a projection created by angry people. Feeling guilty, they assumed they deserved punishment. They therefore concocted the image of a God who would mete out all the punishment they felt they deserved. I can't imagine that any of those people have made it to chapter 3 of this book.

Then there are those who believe in a loving God yet don't understand how such a God would tolerate hungry children, global poverty, and endless wars. Interesting, that, because it's the question He has for us. Hungry children, global poverty, and endless wars are a product of man's misuse of power, not God's.

Created with free will, we can think and do whatever we wish to think and do. God Himself will not save us from the consequences. The Law of Cause and Effect was created for our protection, and He does not violate His own law.

What He will do, and has done, is create the help we need in order that we might choose more wisely. Asking Him to heal the world means asking Him to turn us into the people who will do it for ourselves.

Our relationship to God is, if we allow it to be, our most intimate relationship. His is a voice that is always there to whisper in our ear. He is closer than our breath to us. Our communion with him, our melding into him, is the repair of our personalities and the restoration of our souls. For many, the mystic Jesus is part of that repair.

As far as the hungry children are concerned, this isn't about our waiting for God to work a miracle. God is waiting for us to do that. He has a very simple answer to our prayers about this. His answer is "Feed them."

And we should do so now.

Relationship to Self

Your holiness is the salvation of the world. It lets you teach the world that it is one with you, not by preaching to it, not by telling it anything, but merely by your quiet recognition that in your holiness are all things blessed along with you. (WB-37)

One of our most difficult relationships is our relationship to self. We tend to do to ourselves what we do to others: we withhold approval, judge harshly, punish severely. And we're never too sure why. The ego doesn't tell us we did something wrong; it just tells us that we *are* wrong.

I used to wonder, in my younger, self-hating days, if maybe I'd done something so terrible I'd suppressed it and didn't remember. I couldn't figure out why I felt such disgust toward pretty much everything about myself.

There is a lesson repeated a few times in the *Course*—"I am as God created me"* (T-667)—that says all of us are perfect, unalterable creations in the mind of God. When I first read it, I cried. It formed a crack in what felt like a stone wall in front of my heart. It had never occurred to me that I'm innocent because God created me that way, and my mistakes have not eradicated the divine perfection in which we were all created. God created us perfect because *He* is perfect, and everything created is created in His image. It's such an enormous concept, so infinitely merciful.

There was once a law in various places around the country stating that if a criminal was on the run from police but made their way into a church then they couldn't be arrested. The state was acknowledging that in the eyes of God, we are innocent. In the eyes of God, we are never guilty, because our innocence is Real and our mistakes are not.

But if the real me is eternally innocent, then what about the times when I did something wrong? How do I have a good relationship with myself if I hate something I did? What about the ghostly memories that haunt us in the middle of the night, obsession over mistakes we made years ago, the "if only I'd done this or that" with which we frequently torment ourselves? "If only I hadn't been so stupid" is one of the biggest guns in the ego's arsenal.

One of the absurd faux-spiritual truisms out there is that you can't make a mistake. *Oh, yes, you can*, and some of us have made enough of them to know it. Telling yourself that a mistake was not a mistake, if in fact it was, is not the way to dissolve the guilt you feel because of it.

There is a far more functional, successful way of dealing with this than through trying to suppress our obsessive thoughts. The way to dissolve the self-hatred we feel at such times is through the power of the Atonement.

The Atonement is God's greatest gift, but the choice is given to us whether to activate its power in our lives. This is how it works. You go back to the moment when you made the mistake, and you own it. You look it squarely in the eye; you realize what a lack of love for yourself or others such a moment entailed. You'll see more clearly what was going on with you when you made the mistake.

In such moments in my own past I've come to realize that in those moments I was scared; but I also realized that in those moments I was irresponsible. I either did not know yet or was not practiced yet at asking the Holy Spirit for direction before making my decisions. And in that, I betrayed myself. God was there, but I didn't turn to Him.

Even when we have been most mistaken, the person who we might have been—the way we might have behaved, had the ego not held us in its grip—is an image that has remained in God's mind. Jesus holds this image safe in his hands until we are ready to express it. "I have saved all your kindnesses and every loving thought you ever had. I have purified them of the errors that hid their light, and kept them for you in their perfect radiance"* (T-83).

Living in this world, it can be hard. The ego speaks first and the ego speaks loudest, which is why cultivating our capacity to listen to the small inner Voice for God is so important. I've spent years of my life regretting decisions I would not have made if I had simply given it the weekend to think things through.

The miracle of the Atonement is that you can go back to that moment now. In any situation in which we failed to go for the love—failing to allow the miracle that might have occurred and deflecting a miracle instead—the miracle is held in trust for us until we are ready to receive it. Go back to that moment now. Admit that you made the wrong decision, admit that you didn't let the Holy Spirit guide your thoughts, and ask that it happen now.

Contrition is miraculous. In ways you can't imagine, life will catch up with your change in consciousness. You will have a chance to play life correctly where you might have failed to do so before. A situation will occur that shows you clearly that when you atoned, you were heard.

God is an infinitely merciful God. Yes, we are accountable; but through the grace of God we can begin again.

The section from *A Course in Miracles* that follows is one of its most powerful tools in rewiring the way we perceive the past.

> *... the first step in the undoing is to recognize that you*
> *actively decided wrongly, but can as actively decide otherwise.*
> *Be very firm with yourself in this, and keep yourself fully*
> *aware that the undoing process, which does not come from you,*
> *is nevertheless within you because God placed it there. Your*
> *part is merely to return your thinking to the point at which*
> *the error was made, and give it over to the Atonement in peace.*
> *Say this to yourself as sincerely as you can, remembering that*
> *the Holy Spirit will respond fully to your slightest invitation:*
>   *I must have decided wrongly, because I am not at peace.*
>   *I made the decision myself, but I can also decide otherwise.*
>   *I want to decide otherwise, because I want to be at peace.*
>   *I do not feel guilty, because the Holy Spirit will undo all*
> *the consequences of my wrong decision if I will let Him.*
>   *I choose to let Him, by allowing Him*
> *to decide for God for me.* (T-90)*

All of us have been there. And having made mistakes, of course we suffer. But remorse is a positive thing; only sociopaths are without it. Conscience is an aspect of the heart.

The ego wants to stretch things out, to take the healthy processing of our regrets and turn it into a permanent emotional bludgeon. Once again, the ego is a trick. That does nothing more than delay the day when we go about the business of acting now in a way we didn't act before. If you really want to show God you're sorry, go be a different person now.

Another reason we're sometimes hard on ourselves, of course, is because of the projections of other people. It might be an adult who told you that you were worthless when you were a child, and you've internalized their voice. It might be people who don't even know you, but have created or bought into a false narrative about who you are. Either way, their voices are now inside your head convincing you of your lack of worth.

One of my favorite Christmas carols is "O Holy Night," containing this extraordinary lyric: "Long lay the world in sin and error pining, till He appeared and the soul felt its worth." It doesn't matter who other people think you are. Your inestimable worth is established by God. Yes, we have all made mistakes. But who we are, the innocence in which we were created, is an inviolable essence. What God created cannot be altered. We are perfect ideas in the Mind of God.

Dear God,
I give to you the mistakes of my past.
I recognize that in those moments I did not let love prevail.
May Your Spirit enter my mind, as I
surrender those moments to You.
May my mistake be somehow useful in
making me a better person now.
Amen

Relationship to Others

God loves all of us as one, for He created us as one. Our purpose is to think as God thinks so we can love as He does. We cannot find right relationship to God, or to ourselves, without right relationship to others. The only way we can find peace or love is by giving it to each other, for we *are* each other. It's impossible for me to remember who I am unless I am willing to remember who you are, and it's impossible for me to remember who you are without remembering who I am.

When I told a friend, Andrea, about my experience viewing *Salvator Mundi*, she told me of a similar experience she had had many years ago at Notre Dame Cathedral in Paris. It was similar to mine in that she too felt transported beyond the piece of art, but whereas I saw the realms of tenderness and power, she saw the entirety of the human race. She saw that Jesus was everyone. She saw that we are one.

Relationships are assignments made by the Holy Spirit, part of an intentional plan by which all beings will ultimately be reconciled with God. To be reconciled with God means to be reconciled with the love that is within us. We don't get to God simply by learning to love ourselves. We get to God by learning to love each other.

Relationships are temples of the Holy Spirit* (P-6). They are part of a highly individualized curriculum by which we are each given maximal soul growth opportunities, assigned to those with whom we can both teach and learn.

Relationships are where our strengths are strengthened, and our weaknesses brought up for review. They are where we salute the soul of others or do battle with the soul of others. In intense relationships, we often do both.

Relationships are growth experiences, and life is simply a series of lessons destined to be rehearsed until we learn them fully. You either let go of the past, or string it out and deny yourself and others the chance for a different kind of future.

The Holy Spirit brings us together with people who are perfect matches in terms of not just complementary strengths, but also complementary wounds. That's why relationships are hard. Growth is messy, relationships are messy, and love is messy. An intentional universe nourishes the growth of all living things, and often it's relationships that challenge us to grow.

If we behave unlovingly, we shouldn't expect others to be okay with that. We are responsible for how we present ourselves. Spiritual growth is a path to personal maturity, and the universe will move us along whether we want it to or not. Every relationship, in fact every encounter, gives us the opportunity as well as the challenge to rise to the perfection we're capable of. We can fall into the morass of our ego wounds, but we can also choose not to. Jesus will help us if we ask him to.

How often people abandon one another when the wound is too great and the forgiveness too weak. And sometimes the consequences are tragic. It's often said that love brings up everything unlike itself, the ego never more activated than when two people's hearts are joined. Everything comes up for review and release, no ground more treacherous at times—or more holy—than the ground of love.

Jesus secures our connection to others because he *is* our connection to others. Calling on him is a request for help that rings throughout the universe and is capable of changing it.

Dear Jesus,
Please take into your hands
my relationship with _____.
Lift our relationship to divine right order.
May a wave of forgiveness come upon us both,
dissolving all walls that would divide us. May we
only see the innocence in ourselves and in each
other. Free us of our fears of love, Dear God.
Heal us of our wounds, that we might
no longer wound each other.
Amen

The only way to feel close to God is if we're at least willing to grow closer to people. And obviously that's not always easy. Relating to another human being can be like looking in the mirror and starting to attack the glass. Since on the level of mind there's no separation between us, what we do to others we are doing to ourselves. When we attack anyone, even in our minds, it is as though we are bringing a sword down on their head, but actually it is falling on ours.

This is from *A Course in Miracles*:

A jailer is not free, for he is bound together with his prisoner.
He must be sure that he does not escape, and so he spends his

*time in keeping watch on him. The bars that limit him become
the world in which his jailer lives, along with him. And it is on
his freedom that the way to liberty depends for both of them.*

*Therefore, hold no one prisoner. Release instead of bind,
for thus are you made free. The way is simple. Every time you
feel a stab of anger, realize you hold a sword above your head.
And it will fall or be averted as you choose to be condemned
or free. Thus does each one who seems to tempt you to be
angry represent your savior from the prison house of death.
And so you owe him thanks instead of pain.* (WB-366)*

We become willing to see the innocence in others, then, so that
we might no longer be tempted to attack ourselves. Heaven is an
awareness of our oneness; therefore any thought of lovelessness
toward another denies us the experience of heaven. The peace of
heaven is entered two by two.

If God created me perfect, then that means He created everyone else that way as well. God loves you infinitely, yes, but so too
He loves everyone else. It's difficult for the mortal mind to even
grasp the infinitude of God's love, and Jesus will help us when we
falter. He lifts the mind above thoughts of separation, transcend-
ing fully the thinking of the world, reminding us how to love another person that we might truly love ourselves.

Life's relationship lessons are always occurring. There is no
insignificant encounter because in God's eyes there are no insignificant people. The lesson might be the ethical move we may or
may not be making; the kindness or patience we may or may not
be showing; the person who's helped us toward whom we may
or may not be showing gratitude; the person we may be blaming
when instead we could forgive. Every relationship is a lesson in
learning how to claim, and express, the love that is who we are.

Any time two people join, it will be a holy or an unholy encounter. Either spirit or ego will have its way with us. We'll either meet soul to soul or mask to mask. Our spirits are always leaning toward each other, while our egos are always leaning away.

Yet the choice is always ours. If you're about to meet someone, before you even walk into the room where they are, the most powerful thing you can do is to pray for their happiness. Pray to see their innocence. Pray that God use the relationship for purposes of good. Pray that the relationship blesses both of you, allowing you the opportunity to see each other's innocence. See Jesus with his arms around you both.

This directs your mind to the field you wish to inhabit, the realm of love instead of fear. It sucks the oxygen out of thoughts like "I'm afraid they won't like me." For where there is light there cannot be darkness. Where the mind is attuned to God, it cannot be attuned to neurotic thought. Jesus is a method of attunement. He will lift both of you above the illusion of separation to the field where you are one.

Years ago I was invited to a business meeting with some women in New York. I don't know what made me such an abject failure at all this that day. I don't remember not meditating that morning, although I do remember I came to the meeting straight from the airport. The one thing I do know is that on that day I definitely didn't practice what I preach.

For whatever reason, I had a negative attitude from the moment I entered the room. I even said to someone sitting next to me, "God, I hate meetings like this, don't you?" And that's when I started to see what was happening. I realized that every woman at the table had a look on her face somewhere between shock and serious disappointment. Clearly, they had thought Marianne Williamson wouldn't be like this. They thought I would be . . . well . . . *nicer.*

That was several years ago, and I still feel a pang of embarrassment every time I remember it. One thing it did for me, for sure, was to make me take very seriously how important it is to bless a room before I enter.

As we bless others, we are blessing ourselves. The love we're seeking in life is love that we ourselves must generate. The love we give will be returned to us, and the love we withhold will be withheld from us. We might not see this immediately, but the law is inviolable. Do unto others as you would have others do unto you *because they will*. Or someone else will. An idea doesn't leave its source and what we put out will be returned to us.

Love is always available, but it must be consciously chosen. The ego very slyly resists this, so obsessed with the love we're not getting that little room is left to consider what love we might not be giving. The ego is outraged at the thought that someone might not be loving us perfectly every minute of every day.

Like a scavenger dog, the ego seeks any scrap of evidence of our brother's guilt. Maybe someone didn't fold their laundry correctly! Maybe they had the audacity to disagree with us about something! The ego will use anything to separate us from others. If I'm focused on your guilt, then by definition I'm seeing you as different from me, therefore separate from me. Thus the separation is fortified. Always vigilant on behalf of its survival, the ego is the mind of constant judgment. Literally nothing and no one is ever allowed to be good enough.

It's often only in retrospect that we realize how we blocked love in a relationship; at the time we were so sure the guilty party was the other person, then later realized we ourselves were no better. At the time, we just thought we were setting boundaries! Standing up for ourselves! Refusing to be codependent! In love we are often blind until it's too late. For the ego is our self-hatred often masquerading as self-love. Its insidious dictate in love is "seek but do not find"* (T-343).

All that is why it's important to pray early, at the beginning of a relationship. And then of course to pray without ceasing. I've noticed that when I don't know how to deal with a situation in a loving way—if it triggers me or constricts my heart for whatever reason—as long as I pray, as long as I'm willing to see things differently, Spirit comes rushing to my aid. "I will come in response to a single unequivocal call"* (T-62).

If we're willing to embody more love, opportunities as well as challenges will appear. Whenever you're having a difficult moment in a relationship, stop to ask yourself what you're thinking about this person right now that God would not be thinking, and what God would be thinking about them that you are not. Simply asking the question will summon the answer. God isn't looking at anyone thinking, "Damn, he's such a jerk."

Freud said, "Intelligence will be used in the service of the neurosis"; none of us is too "smart" to fall into the ego's trap when it comes to relationships. The cleverness of our own minds, after all, will be used in the ego's service if we allow it to be. The ego is suspicious at best and vicious at worst. The only way to override it, to dissolve its influence, to cast it back into the nothingness whence it came, is to love so profoundly that it doesn't have a chance.

In moments when it seems too hard, one call and He will be there.

Forgiveness

He will not tell you that your brother should be judged by what your eyes behold in him, nor what his body's mouth says to your ears, nor what your fingers' touch report of him. He passes by such idle witnesses, which merely bear false witness to God's Son. He recognizes only what God loves, and in the holy light of what He sees do all the ego's dreams of what you are vanish before the splendor He beholds.* (WB-278)

We've all been taught the ego's version of forgiveness. Someone else was a jerk, but you (you wonderful thing, you), you're so advanced and spiritually superior that you're willing to forgive them!

Such a perspective is not true forgiveness but rather covert judgment; what a perfect ego concoction. Seeing ourselves as up here and the poor wretch sinner down there, we're simply fortifying the separation. I'm amused when judgmental people say they don't believe in sin. It makes me think, *Oh, yes, you do!* If you believe that guilt is real, you believe in sin.

True forgiveness is the realization that someone's mistake is not who they are. Our willingness to see through the veil of illusion—to extend our perception beyond what our physical senses perceive, to what we know to be true in our hearts—such is the miracle that shifts a relationship on the causal level.

Recently I'd had a back-and-forth with a friend who was annoying me greatly. I wanted to process the issue; she was pulling away and not responding. I'd called once; I'd texted once. I figured anything more and I'd look like a fool.

But I was starting to feel angry and began articulating my attack thoughts in the comfort of my own mind. *Maybe she was using again! Clearly, she wasn't into this friendship anymore! I just know the kinds of people she's hanging out with now, so where is the surprise here?!* I wasn't beyond having such judgmental thoughts, but I was beyond thinking they were sane.

I let my judgmental thoughts boil to the surface, and I simply gave them to God. I knew better than to act on them. But I needed a miracle to calm my anxiety and I prayed for one. *Dear God, please help me see her innocence.*

A couple of hours later I got a text from her. She'd had the flu since last week, she was only starting to feel better, and could she call me tomorrow? She topped it off with a sweet "I love you!"

I hate to admit it even to myself, but there was a time in my life when I might have preempted that miracle with a ridiculous text. The ego claims to be the solution to any anxiety we feel when conflict arises: *Project the blame outward! Tell that person how you feel! Tell them how wrong they are!* The ego doesn't want us to realize, of course, that the attack will boomerang on us.

In fostering guilt in anyone, the ego seeks to cancel out God. The ego constantly seesaws between thoughts of attack and thoughts of defense, both of which foster a belief that someone is guilty and therefore separate from us. Forgiveness reminds us of the eternal innocence in which we were all created. It also reminds us of our oneness with each other, opening our eyes to our spiritual unity. Recognizing our oneness dissolves the ego, because ego is the false belief that we're separate, and it disappears when we see we're not. Where love is, ego cannot be.

Forgiveness means remembering everyone is innocent because God created us that way. All of us lose conscious contact with our innocence at times, living as we do in a world that so contradicts it. But love sees through the illusion of the mistaken self to the truth that lies beyond.

Everyone makes mistakes. Forgiveness has to do with how we respond to them, and how we respond to them has to do with how we interpret them. The miracle-minded interpretation of all human behavior is to see whatever someone did as either love or a call for love. In either case, the appropriate response is love.

When we judge someone, we're holding them hostage to our expectations and standards. But we're holding ourselves hostage as well, for the warden can't leave the prison anymore than the prisoner can. The only way we can free ourselves is if we are willing to free others. What I perceive in you I cannot escape experiencing within myself.

"Forgiveness is a selective remembering, based not on your selection"* (T-354). It is a conscious decision to focus on things that a person did right while our ego is screaming about the thing they did wrong. In the case of my friend—and how often this is true—she hadn't even *done* anything; I just imagined that she had! Forgiveness is a choice to stand on what we know in our hearts, more than on what we perceive with our physical senses.

Forgiving you, I free myself from the effects of whatever lovelessness you had shown me. Choosing not to believe in the cause, I am invulnerable to the effects. And as I choose that miracle in my own life, I become a miracle worker in yours. You are blessed, because my choice to see your innocence reminds you it is there. I am blessed, because in releasing you from guilt I am releasing myself from guilt. Every encounter is a path to heaven or a path to hell, depending on whether I choose for my heart to be open or closed. It is only in choosing to see your innocence that I can see mine.

We cannot experience inner peace if we're holding thoughts of attack against anyone. We can escape the world we don't want only by giving up attack thoughts. Everyone we meet is either our crucifier or our savior, depending on what we choose to be to them.

Forgiveness is both our function and our salvation. It is the only antidote to our war on ourself and others. It is our return to sanity in a world that has gone insane. Forgiveness is an illusion, because it remains within the realm of mortal thought. But it is an illusion that leads beyond illusion. Forgiveness is the way we are set free.

The mystic Jesus *is* the mind of forgiveness. He loves all of us unconditionally because he sees us with the eyes of God. Seeing us with the eyes of God, he sees there is nothing not to love. The miracle of forgiveness is that then we can see it too.

Dear Jesus,
I know yours is the mind of unconditional love,
but of myself I cannot get there.
My wound, my trigger, my pain is too great.
I cannot see the innocence in one who hurt me.
But I am willing,
for I know that in my resistance to love I only hurt myself.
My mind and heart are open to receive you.
Please change my mind and uplift my heart,
that I might love as you do and thus know inner peace.
Amen

Giving Up Grievances

The ego's plan for salvation centers around holding grievances. It maintains that, if someone else spoke or acted differently, if some external circumstance or event were changed, you would be saved. Thus, the source of salvation is constantly perceived as outside yourself. Each grievance you hold is a declaration, an assertion in which you believe, that says, "If this were different, I would be saved." The change of mind necessary for salvation is thus demanded of everyone and everything except yourself.

The role assigned to your own mind in this plan, then, is simply to determine what, other than itself, must change if you are to be saved. According to this insane plan, any perceived source of salvation is acceptable provided that it will not work. This ensures that the fruitless search will continue, for the illusion persists that, although this hope has always failed, there is still grounds for hope in other places and in other things. Another person will yet serve better; another situation will yet offer success.

Such is the ego's plan for your salvation. Surely you can see how it is in strict accord with the ego's basic doctrine: "Seek but do not find."* (WB-121)

Many of us have experienced relationships that felt at some point too hard to heal. Sometimes we've held on to grievances for decades. Yet even the smallest grievance is like a shadow that blocks the sun.

Giving up grievances can be particularly difficult when we feel convinced that the grievance is valid. Then it feels as though by forgiving someone, we're condoning bad behavior. But refusing to forgive someone isn't hurting them; it's hurting you. Do you prefer that you be right or happy?* (T-617).

Most important, by holding grievances, we're keeping the universe from healing whatever situation we were upset by to begin with. We're giving all the power to one we feel hurt by, when the power of God would be ready to fix the situation if only we would get out of the way. The universe is always ready to begin again, to create the next great thing. God can solve any problem the moment the problem occurs. But by carrying grievances from the past into the present, we're preventing Him from doing so. We have to choose to let the miracle in. Our grievances keep us tied to the past, programming the future to be just like it. Only in the Holy Instant, in the space of love that transcends our focus on the past, do our grievances give way to miracles.

Many years ago I had a lunch date with a famous writer whose husband was the editor of a very powerful magazine. There had been an article in the magazine that I felt was demeaning to me, and I felt hurt. I cringe to even think of it now, but I had so little self-discipline that I mentioned my grievance to the woman at lunch.

I saw her face fall and, in that moment, I knew what I had done. I didn't even know yet how badly I had blown it, in fact. I learned afterward that her husband had a very serious cancer; she had read my book, and she had asked to have lunch with me to seek wisdom and counsel. Having not been taken seriously, a situation arose in which I would have been taken seriously indeed. Yet I was the one who deflected that. I showed up as a hurt, petty person dragging the past into the present, and in doing so I blocked the miracle.

According to *A Course in Miracles*, we can have a grievance or a miracle, but we cannot have both. "Holding grievances is an attack on God's plan for salvation"* (WB-124).

Some of the things we need to forgive at times are far, far worse than someone saying something that hurt our feelings. Betrayal, theft, violence—life can be hard, and people can be cruel. Forgiveness can be a process that takes time and doesn't come quickly or easily. But it's a merciful act not only to the other person but to you. The more we hold on to our grievance, the longer it will take for the universe to correct the error and heal our wound.

Forgiving a person doesn't mean we're condoning what they did. And we don't have to worry that by our forgiving them they're going to get away with something either. Divine justice is inviolable; the universe keeps a perfect set of books. The saying "Vengeance is mine, sayeth the Lord" means the problem is God's to handle, not yours. Our punishing attitudes do nothing to serve the process by which someone is held accountable; revenge will only boomerang on us.

Many times when we're most angry at what someone did to us, the hate we don't want to look at is really toward ourselves: a realization of what we ourselves had done, or not done, to contribute to the situation that hurt us. In what ways had we made it easy for someone to do what they did? In what ways did we not show up for ourselves? We can't always control what has happened in our lives, but we can always control who we choose to be once it happens. The crucifixion might not have been our choice, but the resurrection always is.

Love is the solution no matter the problem. It doesn't matter whether our conflict is with someone we're only thinking about, or someone we've been married to for decades. The principle is the same. In separating ourselves from someone else, we're separating ourselves from God. And in separating ourselves from God, we're blocking a miracle and sabotaging ourselves.

If there is someone you are having a hard time forgiving, this will help you...

Get comfortable and close your eyes...

Now with your inner eye, on the left side of your vision, see the other person as they normally appear to you. See their body, their clothes, their behavior as you know it.

Focus on that image for a moment, then see a little ball of golden light begin to form in the area of their heart. Now slowly see the light expand until it covers every cell of their body. Again, going slowly, allow yourself to see the light expand beyond the confines of their body, shining so brightly that the physical body itself fades into shadow. See the light as it extends outward, beyond their skin and all around them.

Again, very slowly, move your inner eye to the right side of your vision and see yourself. Look at yourself, your body, your clothes, how you express yourself behaviorally. Now see in the middle of your heart that little ball of golden light. Watch it cover every cell and organ of your body. Watch your body fade into shadow. Again, very slowly, watch the light expand beyond the confines of your body, making the physical body itself move into shadow. Watch as the light extends outward, beyond your body and in every direction. Now...

Very slowly, look to the center where the light

extending from the other person merges with the light
extending from you. There, in that golden light, beyond
the body, is the temple of your holy relationship.

Simply stay there. Do not move your inner
eye. Bear witness. Be still and know.

Allow yourself to recognize that point of oneness
which is the reality of spirit, beyond the body,
beyond separation, and thus beyond guilt.

You are at home now, in each other and in God.

Dear God,
I place in Your hands my relationship with _____.
Lift us above the walls that would divide us.
May a great wave of forgiveness come upon us both,
washing away the thoughts of guilt
that would destroy our love.
May our eyes be opened to the innocence
in ourselves and in each other.
May our relationship be lifted to divine right order,
a blessing upon us both,
in whatever form You would appoint.
Amen

Relationship to the World

When one of the kindest, most sensitive women I've ever known died in one of the airplanes on September 11, I realized that all of us, no matter who we are or where we are, are affected by international affairs. None of us can completely seal ourselves off from the world. We're all increasingly vulnerable to global dysfunction, whether climate change or nuclear risks or economic uncertainty. The only way to take responsibility for our lives now is to take responsibility for the world.

When I was in the seventh grade, I came home one day and told my parents we had to fight in Vietnam or we would be fighting on the shores of Hawaii. I had learned about the "domino theory" that day in school, and I began to instruct my parents about what it meant. I saw the muscles on my father's face begin to tighten. I saw my mother put her hand over her eyebrow, like, *Uh oh, here we go.*

After listening for several minutes, my father stood up from the dinner table. "That's *it*, sweetheart!" he said to my mother. "We're going to Vietnam."

That was 1965; you could still visit Saigon as long as you stayed within five miles of the city. But there was a fear, a tension in the air, a sense of doom that was palpable. I remember my father showing us bullet holes on the side of a building and talking to us about how they got there.

He sat us down on a bench next to him and said, "Hear me and never forget this, kids. These are real people. If anyone ever tries to convince you that these people don't matter, that we can go to war against anyone when it isn't necessary, promise me you will remember this trip. Some of the people you have met here might not survive what is about to happen."

He was right, of course. I did and I do remember. There's a certain invulnerability to propaganda that I and my brother and sister carried with us. It's been a shield against the official malarkey so often used to enroll us in agreeing to do what we should not do.

Jesus loves the world, and we should love it too. The ego loves to say that loving one another "has nothing to do with politics," but of course it would say that. It lies. In the words of Mahatma Gandhi, "Is not politics a part of dharma too?" If God's love applies to our relationship to everything, then that means it applies to our relationship to the world at large. And our relationship to the world at large can't be separated from politics.

When I was growing up there was a huge atlas that we kept in our family's den. My father used to show us the geographic map of the world and point out, "Look, kids, God didn't create lines between countries. We did." That which separates us is by definition man-made.

For centuries, the Ukrainian and Russian people lived like brothers. Similarly, the people of Texas and Mexico have been peacefully crossing over into each other's territories for centuries.

Arabs and the Jews were nomadic friends for even longer. The modern nation-state is often a transactional separation of peoples whose hearts have been historically unified. The ego works on a collective as well as an individual level, always seeking to separate, to destroy the fragile bonds that unite us. Our task is to create a world in which appropriate boundaries are reflective of a higher order of civilization, not a barbaric display of disunity. We must find a way to determine our borders without closing our hearts.

In alchemy there is a term, "separatio," which means separating out all the elements in order to purify them, allowing for their rearrangement at a higher level. Our different ethnicities, cultures, nationalities, sexual and gender identities, religions, and so forth are magnificent kaleidoscopic expressions of one internal truth. They are beautiful points on the rim of the wheel, but they are not the mystical hub. They are not the deepest truth of who we are. On the level of the deepest truth we are one, and our purpose on this earth is to learn to live that way.

The ego will always strive to keep us separate, and the suffering engendered by its investment in guilt is intense and ongoing. People die to preserve the illusion of separation, and God doesn't look away from such suffering. Jesus wept, and so should we.

We should weep for others, and we should weep for ourselves, for we will reap what we have sown. Collectively as well as individually, the time for a massive Atonement is at hand. The Law of Cause and Effect means karma, and ours is not so very good. From the violence we show to each other, to violence against other countries, to violent transgression against the earth itself, our collective ego is doing what the ego does. Its goal is not to inconvenience, but to destroy.

At this point, many wonder, is it even possible to begin again?

As a species, can we change? Can we heal? The answer is absolutely yes. We can atone for our errors, make restitution, and reform our ways. That is as true for a nation as it is for a person.

We will learn to live together in love. We will learn it through wisdom, or we will learn it through pain. But we will learn.

Soul Growth

Spirituality is not something to be practiced *sometimes*. It is the existential meaning of every moment. The spiritual journey is continuous and practical. It is a moment-by-moment decision-making process: How do I choose to look at a situation, who do I choose to be within it, and what do I choose to do?

Life is about not just what happens to us, but also who we choose to be in the space of what happens. Every situation is designed by an intelligent universe specifically for our soul growth, by definition presenting us with the opportunities to play life either from a place of love or from a place of fear—from forgiveness, positivity, and contribution, or from blame, negativity, and victimhood.

Every moment we make the choice. We make it either consciously or unconsciously, but every thought represents a decision, and "All thinking produces form at some level"* (T-31). That is how powerful we are, and how responsible we are for our life experience.

The life we live is a reflection of thoughts we chose to think before this moment. Our lives begin to change when we choose to think differently now. The spiritual journey is a transition from who we used to be and the life we used to live, to who we would rather be and the life we would rather live. No one and nothing can decide for you the thoughts you choose to think.

The world would tell us there's no road map, nothing but a random universe in which the highest good is to do whatever we feel like doing, or would make us the most money, or would get us whatever it is we think we want. Nothing is a more limited mentality than such a purposeless perspective.

Living our lives in service to a *higher* purpose is the only road to happiness, because it is the reason we were born. What the ego posits as freedom is not freedom, but license; it is a prison of our own making. Following Jesus, serving the Will of God, trying our best to be loving means serving the desires of our own true self.

The Pillars of a
Well-Lived Life

The three principles we hold on to as we walk the spiritual path are these: faith, love, and service.

Those are the pillars of righteousness, or "right use-ness" of the mind. But even more than that, they are our powers. They are the use of the mind in ways that lift us above the normal limitations of the mortal world.

Who among us has not seen things come together when harmony exists among the players in a system, and things fall apart when anger and negativity prevail?

Our faith that anything is possible in the presence of love, our faith that forgiveness will always interrupt the ego's tyranny—these are our powers when we let miracles light the way. The Holy Spirit is the motivation for miracles and conduit for miracles. He is never not available to show us where they are. "I am not absent to anyone in any situation" (T-116).

The world can be a miraculous place, and in many ways it is. We hold our children, we fall in love, we build communities. It's all there. But the fear-based thought system that dominates the world is like a sword of Damocles that hangs above us all. The fate of our world literally hangs on whether or not we can stop attacking each other, attacking the earth, and attacking ourselves.

We need faith that it's possible for us, and for the world, to change.

We need love to dissolve the layers of fear that saturate the world.

We need a consciousness of service to make sure we will.

As we increase our ability to embody the love that is the truth of who we are, we begin to attract mighty companions into our experience. We meet people with whom there's an almost mysterious sense that we were brought together for purposes higher than our own. We're no longer driven to achieve what we perceive to be our separate goals, but instead we're driven by a desire to collaborate with others in creating collective changes to the world in which we live.

The idea that we go to work to make money, to gain power, or for any other purpose dictated by a consumer-driven culture begins to take second place to a more meaningful yearning: to create the good, the beautiful, and the holy. And to create those things with others.

The intentional nature of the universe applies not only to our individual lives but to our relationships as well. We are drawn to people with whom we can heal and with whom we can create more than we could have created on our own. This is the regenerative energy of Christ that is emerging in the world today. Yes, the ego's wiles are still a danger to us all. But the sense that God is active, that the spirit of rebirth is upon us, that Jesus walks on the water even now, is palpable as well.

He is order in the midst of chaos, he is wisdom in the midst of confusion, he is the love that casts out fear. Jesus is in you and me and all of us, by whatever name we call him. In moments of despair we need but call, and he will hear, and he will answer. The times ahead might indeed be challenging, but we will not be alone.

Love will prevail, for God always gets the final say. What is completely up to us, to be determined by the exercise of our free will, is how long it will take to get there—and how much suffering must occur before the dawning of the light. In the Talmud it is written that in the midst of the darkest night we should act as if morning has already come. For in a way it already has.

Hallelujah. Praise God. Amen.

CHAPTER FOUR

HE DID NOT DIE

Teach not that I died in vain. Teach rather that I did not die, by demonstrating that I live in you.* (T-209)

Jerusalem

The Church of the Holy Sepulchre in the Old City of Jerusalem contains two of the holiest sites in Christianity: the place where Jesus was crucified, and the tomb where his body was taken and from which he resurrected.

It's rather shocking how much history is recorded there, based on traditions going all the way back to the fourth century. Visitors walk up a narrow flight of stairs to see the actual site of the crucifixion; in a room right below, behind glass, one can see the rock onto which his blood was spilled. To me, one of the most profound parts of the Bible is the story of women gathered around the foot of the cross and refusing to abandon him in the hours of his suffering.

Being in the church is very moving, and I had an interesting experience the first time I went. A friend and fellow student of *A Course in Miracles* named Daniella happened to be in Israel while I was there, and we had spoken on the phone that morning. She was in Tel Aviv and I was in Jerusalem, both of us busy with various things and not knowing at what point we'd be in the same town. We were going to continue to communicate, making sure we'd have a chance to visit sometime during the week I was there.

Visiting the church several hours later, I was overwhelmed by how many hundreds of people were milling around. Tourists and disciples from all over the world visit the church in every hour that it's open–four million people annually–and the hustle and bustle of so many people in every corner of every room is simply part of the experience.

After I'd gone upstairs and come back down again, I headed for the lower room beneath where Jesus had died. Upstairs is where they say he was crucified; downstairs is where those who bore witness to his suffering were gathered. Looking in, I saw to my surprise that the room was entirely empty. Empty, that is, except for Daniella.

I looked at her and she looked at me. No words could have matched the moment. Both of us felt it. I don't know who was at his feet two thousand years ago, but Daniella and I were at his feet together now.

Detroit

The modern mind is prone to scoffing at the idea of evil, capable of acknowledging its existence but considering itself too smart to investigate its source. The ego loves that attitude, of course. It enables the ego to operate in secret.

The ego is not a dysfunction, it is a malfunction. It is not neutral, it is malevolent. And its goal is not to inconvenience you; its goal is to destroy anything beautiful and precious you have ever known, including you.

Jesus died a horrible death, not some quick mortal wound but rather a torture that went on for hours. With every hour his suffering increased. There could be no more potent image of injustice and unmitigated cruelty than the torture of an innocent man who had helped many and harmed no one.

It is not the reality of his death, but the meaning of his death, that is meant to instruct us. Billions of people suffer no less horribly, and no less unfairly, on the earth today. In recognizing the suffering of Jesus, we should remember the suffering of the world. His message wasn't "Hey, look at me." His message is "Hey, look at you."

Many years ago I was the minister at a nondenominational church and spiritual center in Detroit. When I first arrived, I was told it was a tradition there to celebrate a Good Friday service. I hesitated; I am not a Christian minister but a teacher of universal spiritual truths. I could eagerly talk about Easter and the Resurrection. But a Good Friday service had a uniquely Christian ring to it, and I didn't know if it was something I could do.

I realized that the Good Friday service meant a lot to the congregants, so I looked more deeply into it. I came to see more clearly the spiritual and psychological connection between acknowledging the death of Jesus on Friday and celebrating his resurrection on Sunday. I have never been interested in religious dogma, but I'm interested in the religious experience, and there's nothing more profound than a religious service when it's authentic and real. The word "religion" comes from the Latin root "religio," which means to bind back. Its purpose is to bind us back to the truth in our hearts.

What began as something I resisted became for me the most powerful day of the year during my tenure at Renaissance Unity. For one day, at one service, we acknowledged the depth of human suffering, both our own and that of others. We felt the horror and the grief and the pain of this world. We stood before it and did not look away. We took it in, we did not ignore it. Bearing witness to the suffering of Jesus, we bore witness to the suffering of the world.

When Sunday arrived, we weren't just dressed up fancy on Easter morning. We didn't just bliss out on the gospel choir singing hallelujah. No, something very important had occurred at that Good Friday service, and we had all experienced it. We were able to take in the joy of Easter in a way we could not have otherwise; having allowed ourselves to truly see what becomes of a world in which love is absent, we could celebrate its reappearance in a whole new way.

Having gazed deeply into the darkness of the crucifixion, we then gazed more deeply into the light of the resurrection. We don't heal our wounds by ignoring them. The crucifixion is the wound of the world—the ego's violent, destructive force in whatever form it appears. If you don't look at it at all, you're not in transcendence but in denial. Look at it, and then consider that in Jesus the lesson has been learned. Through the power of the resurrection, the effects of darkness are nullified.

He has overcome, and so can we.

Crucifixion

The suffering of Jesus on the cross was a historical event, of course, but like all aspects of his life on earth it speaks to our reality now. His suffering was an embodiment of the full viciousness of the ego in order for God to demonstrate, through the resurrection, that there is no evil in the world that God's love does not nullify.

While traditionalists believe that the suffering of Jesus ransomed a sinful humanity, esoteric teachings argue otherwise. The crucifixion was not a punishment for anything or anyone. A loving God would not have Jesus die because *you* were bad.

Rather, we can see the crucifixion of Jesus as the last useless journey, the final detour into the regions of darkness. Among his final words were "It is finished." He was speaking not only for himself but for all of us. He had taken on the darkness of the world, even unto death itself, and he survived. United with the consciousness of an eternal God, he was deathless. In the realm of spirit, so are we.

But Jesus is not asking us to join in his crucifixion; he is asking us to join in his resurrection. The crucifixion was a radical demonstration of how far the ego will go; the resurrection is a radical demonstration of God's power to override it. It is proof that while hatred *apparently* triumphed over love, in time love would have the final say.

As with everything else in the life of Jesus, the principle revealed in the crucifixion applies to all of us. Our crucifixions are rarely as extreme as his, of course, yet the pattern by which ego seeks to destroy the spirit is as operative in our own lives as it was in his. The point, again, is to claim the power of the resurrection. No matter what we're going through, love will divinely correct all things. The mind of Jesus cracked the code. In joining our minds with his, we crack it too.

Sometimes the crucifixion is something as small as an unkind act or hurtful comment from someone. Yet even the smallest annoyance is good practice, an opportunity to choose to rise above. The accumulation of many smaller wounds can be enough to harden us. A little ego is still ego. It's like a little bit of cancer. Best it were not there.

The crucifixion is a constant reenactment of the ego's ever-vigilant efforts to attack, to destroy, and to kill. The ego tempts us constantly to think thoughts that would destroy our peace, sabotage our relationships, and deflect the miracles that are our divine inheritance. It is the insanity and fear that prevails upon the planet, the malignant consciousness of a humanity having forgotten both our source and our purpose. We have become deeply confused and have forgotten who we are. The ego is literally anti-God. It seeks to attack us, vilify us, and ultimately destroy us.

The crucifixion of Jesus is the ultimate symbol of the ego having gotten its wish, causing us to suffer and ultimately to die. The ego is the belief that we are our bodies; therefore to the ego the death of the body is the ultimate triumph.

Our triumph over death lies in the realization that the dead do not die. For what God created cannot be uncreated. As God's creations, we are eternal spirits, and what lives in God cannot die. His creations are unchangeable and unassailable.

The message of the crucifixion was not that Jesus died. The message is that he did not die. He continues to live, and he lives in us.

All of It Is Happening Now

Crucifixion and resurrection aren't just symbols; they are spiritual dynamics that underly our thoughts, feelings, and experiences. Fear depresses us, while love uplifts us. This is the existential loom onto which we weave our lives.

In every instant we choose crucifixion or resurrection, fear or love. In any moment the ego will have its way with us, and in any moment we can rise above.

The ego crucifies by separating us from each other, which is why we cannot be joined in crucifixion. We are joined in resurrection, for it is the realization that we cannot *be* separated. Every thought of guilt is the nail by which we crucify, and every thought of forgiveness is the power by which we resurrect. Guilt is the cornerstone of the ego's thought system, just as innocence is the cornerstone of the Holy Spirit's.

In projecting guilt onto someone else, we are attacking ourselves. Like an autoimmune disease, the ego insanely attacks that which we are meant to bless. Given that the power of the mind is literally infinite, it becomes an instrument of mass destruction more powerful than any we can imagine.

I remember having dinner with my daughter when she was about ten years old. I don't know how the topic came up, but somehow there was a mention of nuclear bombs. I remember her putting her little head in her hands and saying with great intensity, "The fact that they exist is *insane.*"

She said it with a moral clarity that only a child can express— simple and unequivocal. There were not yet mitigating factors, complicated justifications, or any excuses whatsoever that could veil the absolute truth in her mind. And she was right.

The issue is not that nuclear bombs are good or bad. The issue is that they are *insane.* Given that enough of them could destroy human civilization as we know it, or possibly even the species for at least a few hundred thousand years, the very fact that they exist is an example of how humanity crucifies itself. When Gandhi said that the problem of the world is that humanity is not in its right mind, he was right.

Yet we can choose again. We can be as vigilant against the ego as for it. The resurrection having already been accomplished, the issue is whether or not we choose to claim it. Resurrection is a choice.

We live in a world in which crucifixion is given more respect than love. We have more faith in the power of cancer to kill us than we have in God to heal us. How much more attention and resources are given to those who know how to wage war and man- ufacture the means to do it, than to those who know how to wage peace and build thriving communities? We literally give more respect to fear than to love. Our collective ego uses all manner of pseudosophistication to obscure its real intentions. The way of resurrection is available; it's simply too often unchosen.

Jesus having already broken the spell of darkness, the res- urrection is now an established fact in the ethers of human consciousness. It's like a superpower we just leave lying on the sidewalk. Saying we believe in the resurrection yet refusing to live its message, we simply mock Jesus as he was mocked before.

And what is our resistance? Why, with so many professing our desire to love and to be loved, do we so often not? Surely it is not because love is unreasonable. According to *A Course in Miracles*, love restores reason and not the other way around.

No, our resistance is about something deeper than that. Our resistance is the fact that the one thing we find scarier than death is the prospect of having to change. Some people would rather die than change their mind* (MT-51). If Jesus is real, if he is alive and his power is available to us, then basically everything we've ever been taught about the world is untrue. And that's true—but also terrifying to the ego.

The ego is terrified of love, and our identification with ego has made us terrified of love too. The belief that we are separate is so ingrained into our thought system that we fear annihilation without it. That's because to the ego, love *is annihilation*.

Those who profess love as the cure to the world's ailments are so often deemed "not in touch with reality." The reality we don't *choose* to be in touch with is a reality that will kill us all. Even more significantly than that, the ego's reality isn't even ultimate reality. Humanity is awakening from the real to the Real.

From climate change that could make the planet uninhabitable for most people, to prospects of nuclear disaster, our current way of living on this planet is a slow-moving crucifixion of the human race.

But the story isn't over. Resurrection is a choice.

Tomb Time

Sometimes we crucify ourselves, while at other times we're crucified by others. We've felt at times like we were cast into a darkened cave, our hopes and dreams having been shattered in front of us. We feel the ego has won; we're done; we're defeated. All hope is lost; the anxiety mounts. Such is the crucifixion of self.

Sometimes the crucifixion is individual, as in the perpetration of a wrong committed against one person; at other times, the crucifixion is collective, such as war or genocide committed against a group of people. The crucifixion is a universal experience. It relates as much to the suffering of humanity today as it related to the suffering of Jesus on the cross two thousand years ago.

Jesus on the cross is the symbol of fear's rampage and the suffering it produces. Whatever the form or size, the crucifixion is always an example of the consciousness of fear seeking to obliterate the consciousness of love. The crucifixion was a sign that apparently fear had won.

But *only* apparently. For the ego's win was temporary. Three days after the crucifixion, the women who arrived to retrieve the body of Jesus were told it was no longer there. They were met by angels who told them, "He is risen." His being had been transformed.

The three days between the crucifixion and the resurrection are psychologically significant. They symbolize the time it takes for a pattern of fear to transform into a pattern of love. It is the time it takes for forgiveness to shift our consciousness and rearrange our circumstances. The way we *think* while we are in the middle of a crucifixion determines our power to invoke the resurrection.

If Jesus had closed his heart or lost his faith, the resurrection would not have occurred. He placed his mind so fully in the hands of God that all power of God was given unto him. He doubted, perhaps, but he did not waver.

What does it mean to waver? It means to give in to hatred, anger, resentment, victimization, revenge, or any other closed-hearted response to the crucifixions in our lives. Lovelessness deflects the miracle by which the universe would otherwise self-correct. While such feelings might be thoroughly valid, even in the midst of our tears we can say, "I am willing to see this differently."

Knowing that *nothing real can be threatened* and *nothing unreal exists* is the thought that casts out darkness. We don't wait until we feel that way to embrace the thought; we embrace that thought, which begins to alchemize our feelings. If something is not love, it exists within the three dimensions yet has no ultimate reality. As we embrace the knowledge of what's Real, what is unreal begins to lose its hold on us.

During that time, it makes sense that we're in grief over the conditions that hurt us. But knowing the deeper significance of that time period gives us the power to hasten its end. It gives us faith. It gives us the ability to see the victory that is as yet unseen. It gives us the strength to endure, to know that "this too shall pass."

None of this is always easy and sometimes it's very hard.

It doesn't take a lot of work to complain, but it does take a lot of work sometimes to burn through the pain and hold on to our faith. Faith in things unseen is like flying on instruments, when a pilot knows the horizon is there but simply can't see it through the clouds. Faith is the realization that no matter what tears we're crying now, we're in the process of an awakening that will lead us to a peaceful place. We can't see that when our spiritual eyes are not yet open. Jesus will lend us his, if we ask.

In the meantime, we don't deny our tears. They are part of the healing process. Women wept at the feet of the crucified Jesus, and so do we.

Tomb time, as my friend Sandhi calls it, is sacred in its own way. It's important to surround ourselves at such times with people who have compassion for our suffering, yet refuse to join in an interpretation of events that would only prolong it. It's the meaning of the Simon & Garfunkel lyric, "Hello darkness, my old friend, I've come to talk with you again." Tomb time is often a period of deep sadness—over a divorce, a poor diagnosis, the loss of a loved one, and so on—and we cannot rush through it. The time to be heartbroken is when our heart is breaking.

There's a way in which, given the state of the world today, being heartbroken—sharing in the sentiment "Jesus wept" in response to the suffering of the world—is not only legitimate, it is healthy. It is a functional response to the sorrow of our times, not a dysfunctional one. If anything, our denying how far off course humanity has swerved—our trying to suppress the pain and even calling our heartbreak a "syndrome"—*that* is pathological. Nothing would be better for humanity right now than if we could all together have a big, long cry. Good Friday is that, in a way. Or that is what it should be.

He Did Not Die

Going through the pain of life, even its extreme pain, and allowing Jesus to impress himself upon your mind while you do, invokes the resurrection in your life as in his. He will mystically overshadow you during your time of heartbreak. He will share his resurrection with you.

The fact that you hold on to love while having endured a crucifixion—that you are willing to forgive, that you continue to serve, that you have faith in miracles—is your salvation and rebirth. You will literally no longer be who you used to be, having been transformed and illumined by your pain. The emotional body of your broken self, like the physical body of Jesus, will disappear. The women at the tomb being told that his body had disappeared means your defeated personality will no longer exist. Your persona will shift. You will become someone new. *You will no longer be who you used to be.*

He rose, and so shall you.

Easter

Christmas and Easter are like existential bookends that hold the psyche together. They relate not only to events in the past but also to the meaning of every moment. In any instant we can give birth to Christ through the expression of our love, and in any situation we can overcome the darkness of the world through the expression of our love. Jesus is the Alpha and the Omega because his mind is both the beginning and the end of everything.

Easter is the good news because it's the ultimate triumph of spirit over matter. The purpose of the crucifixion was not to perpetuate suffering but to end it. Jesus doesn't invite you to take up his cross, *but to put down yours.*

It's not that we are asked to ignore our problems. We should look at our crucifixions but not dwell on them. If we simply ignore a problem, we're not in transcendence but in denial. If we overemphasize the problem, however, we increase its power over us. The art of living lies in acknowledging the existence of the crucifixion—the ego, the fear, the destructiveness it causes—yet denying its power over us. That *is* the resurrection: not just the gentleness of love, but also the power of love.

The power of the resurrection is a power in each of us; the issue is not that our power is weak, but that our faith is weak. We often have more faith in the power of a problem than we have faith in the power of God to solve it. That's why faith matters; it is a power of the mind. And miracles arise from conviction. Conviction is a force multiplier. Standing with conviction that the power of love is greater than the power of fear creates a portal through which miracles flow.

Jesus did not say he had fixed the world; he said he had overcome it. His consciousness was lifted above attachment to the world, and therefore its cruelty could not ultimately destroy him. We say to darkness: "Yes, I see you, but I deny your power to defeat me. I claim the power of the overcoming. Jesus robbed you of your power; therefore you have no power over me."

Because all minds are joined, when anyone achieves anything, then their achievement becomes an available option for everyone. Jesus having broken the ego's spell, it is now broken for anyone who chooses to place their mind under his guidance.

The ego is literally a misunderstanding. Its biggest falsehood is that our lives are limited to the life of the body. It is the illusion that we are temporary beings when the life of the spirit is eternal. Overcoming that illusion is the miracle that sets us free.

In fact, the body is like a suit of clothes. "Physical birth is not a beginning; it is a continuing" (T-81). And physical death is not an ending; it is a continuing as well.

Death, according to the ego, is proof that we are locked into the body, destined to suffer and doomed to die. But if death is in fact not the end of our lives, then we are liberated from all manner of limited beliefs. We are freed from the idea that we are separate, and we are freed from the belief that we are tied to the limitations of the mortal plane. The ego mind is trapped within illusions of the material world in ways the mystic mind transcends.

A mystical understanding of Easter is the furthest thing in the world from a simplistic, merely symbolic image of hope of better things to come. It is a description of reality more advanced than our minds can yet comprehend. As our actualized potential, Jesus is ahead of us. He's showing us what is possible. He's showing us what will yet be ours.

There's no reason to mimic his suffering when we can celebrate, and share, his resurrection. He didn't come to deliver the *bad* news, after all. He is not looking for us to reiterate the suffering that he came to earth to eradicate. He is looking to us to reflect his teaching that a better way is possible.

Demonstrating what he does through us is how we demonstrate what he did for us. We teach miracles by working miracles, overcoming in our own way the wounds that have stricken us, the forces that would limit us, and the fears that would stymie us. As we rise above our own crucifixions, he continues to overcome through us.

Violence Against God

Crucifixion is the ego's violence against God, against love, against you. It takes many forms, often subtle and difficult to decipher. In a phrase used in Alcoholics Anonymous, it is both "cunning and baffling." It is your own mind turned against you.

We all know that thievery, violence, murder, and so forth are evil and wrong. What we don't necessarily realize is that snarkiness, derision, purposeful disrespect, arrogance, self-righteousness, selfishness, and condescension are nests in which such evils fester. The fact that the vast majority of people would never steal, behave violently, or murder is obviously not enough to create a world in which such things do not occur. The only way to defeat evil is to stop it at its source. The ethers of the world are saturated with the origins of the most horrible things imaginable.

We are living at a time when some of the most horrible things imaginable have now become commonplace. They appear to be distinct and separate incidents, unrelated to each other, and on the material plane perhaps they are. But tracing their cause goes back to underlying collective issues. Cruelty leveled against a child can lead in time to cruelty on the part of the adult they become. A traumatized child is likely to become a traumatized adult. The crucified give pain because they are in pain* (T-424).

Since all minds are joined, each of us in every moment has the chance to purify the ethers of the world. We ourselves, in our own lives, help invoke the resurrection that helps uplift the world. There is no large or small contribution to the purification of the collective. The macro matters, and the micro matters too; spiritually they are all the same. Miracles are not quantifiable, for they emerge from a realm beyond time and space. As such, they affect situations we will never even know about* (T-6). When you forgive someone in one part of the world, you could be affecting a situation thousands of miles away.

The closer we grow to God, the closer we grow to our natural desire to help heal others. No serious spiritual path gives anyone a pass on addressing the suffering of other sentient beings. We don't get to say, "Well, the world is screwed, but all I can do is heal my one little life, and that's enough." All of us are responsible for all of us, since all of us *are* all of us.

The crucifixion relates as much to the suffering of humanity today as it related to the suffering of Jesus on the cross two thousand years ago. He didn't resurrect just for you or for me; he resurrected for the world.

The Christ in You
Cannot Be Crucified

Since only love is real and nothing else exists, the real you cannot *be* crucified. The Christ in you is invulnerable to the machinations of the ego, in others or even in yourself. Perfect love is unassailable.

The body can be destroyed, but the spirit cannot. Your ego can be bruised, but your spirit cannot be touched. That is why clarity about who we *are* is the key to our experience of life.

Several years ago, I went to see a one-woman play in which the writer and actor made a rude remark about me as part of her performance. I was shocked, because I'd had no idea such a thing was coming. I had actually thought I was attending the play to be supportive. My feelings were hurt, and I felt publicly humiliated.

As I walked out of the theater, a friend I was with said, "Please call me this week if you want to process this. I know you must feel terribly hurt." I did, and it was important that I not deny that feeling–but as I began to respond to my friend's offer, this quote from the *Course* popped clearly into my head: "It is not Christ that can be crucified"* (WB-451).

Yes, Marianne, your human personality can get all bent out of shape about this. You can even milk it if you want to. *Gee, you can even post about it!*

But my spirit literally could not have cared less, for the spirit is untouched by lovelessness. I could drag this out or I could rise right now. I could identify with victimhood, or I could identify with victory. My choice was whether to identify with my Self or with my ego.

Remembering that the spirit can't be crucified, I realized I had a choice how to move through my hurt feelings. I had learned there's a difference between feeling our feelings and coddling them. I surrendered the experience, including my hurt and humiliation, to God.

I walked back into the theater to head to the ladies' room before we left, and in the hallway I ran into a woman I hadn't seen in a while.

"Hi!" I said. "Good to see you!"

"Good to see you too!" she said. "I produced the play. Did you like it?"

"Well, actually, no," I demurred. "That line about me really hurt my feelings..." I didn't say it as an attack. I was just honestly answering her question.

"I don't blame you," she said. "I had asked her to take out that line. I'm sorry."

I appreciated her understanding and asked what she thought I should do. She told me she thought I should send an email to the writer/actor of the play. I lived with the hurt for a bit, but also stayed prayerful and asked God to help me see this differently. After a day or two I did feel moved to write the email.

Everything we do is infused with the consciousness with which we do it, and I knew that if I communicated from my wound then

He Did Not Die

I would exacerbate the wound. If I communicated like a victim, I would only fortify my victimization. "The sole responsibility of the miracle worker is to accept the atonement for himself"* (T-25). Our first and most important work in any situation is to correct our own perception.

Making God our primary relationship puts us in our right mind; only then can we heal with others. This wasn't about *her* lesson; it was about mine. In writing to her, I was very careful not to blame or attack. I simply shared my hurt and said that the slight seemed to me gratuitous and unnecessary. It was one of those situations where I read the email to a friend, draft after draft, until he said, "Yep, you've got it now. No barbs. Okay to send."

Linda kindly wrote back and apologized, something I don't think would have occurred had I gone on the attack. Most important, she changed the script. That situation was a bit of a miracle in my life—a small one perhaps, and personal to me, but when we see such principles in action we learn to apply them more universally.

All of us get our feelings hurt sometimes, and it's not an experience to suppress or gloss over. But neither is it a feeling we have to make more of than it is. The way of the miracle worker is to place such feeling in the hands of God. A spiritual alchemy then lifts us above the lower emotions that would perpetuate the cycle of pain.

Often we feel we're hurt because of what someone else did when their hearts were closed to us. But in reality, what happened was that their having closed their heart to us then tempted us to close our heart to them. And *that* is what hurts. I saw an interview with a Tibetan monk who had been tortured and imprisoned by agents of the Chinese government. When asked what his greatest fear had been, he said it was that he would give in to his temptation to hate those who tortured him. Redemption lies in refusing to close our hearts to anyone, even when they have closed their heart to us. No matter what other people choose to do, our power lies in how we choose to interpret what they do. When we see lovelessness as a call for love, we rise.

The consciousness of a mind surrendered to God, even for a moment, has the power to work miracles. Jesus did not speak of hate for his accusers or blame those around him. He loved even those who hated him. His mind was so purely aligned with the unconditionally loving spirit of God that all the power of God was given unto him.

We don't have to be spiritual masters to diminish the ego's power in our lives. Each of us is responsible for what we choose to think. If I only identify with my body, then I'm identifying with my weakness and will interpret the world in a way that fortifies my weakness. If I identify with my spirit, then I am identifying with my strength and will interpret the world in a way that fortifies my strength.

This was one of so many times in my life when I've been served by the thought, *Oh, Marianne, get over yourself. Your life will be so much better if you do.*

Sickness

The Christ in you is not a body. The body, when properly perceived, is seen as a suit of clothes. The spirit is eternal, while the body is dust to dust.

Overidentification with the body puts a stress on the body that it was not meant to carry. The most powerful view of the body is one in which we realize that it's not the ultimate reality of who we are.

Understanding right relationship between body and mind is a key element in the spiritual evolution of the planet. The body is meant to be servant to the mind, not the other way around. When in right relationship, the spirit enlivens the body and supports the healthy functioning of the immune system. It is literally our life force.

Jesus is like a carpenter's balance, aligning our perceptions in such a way as to support our highest functioning while on earth. The Holy Spirit enters into the realm of the body at the level of our receptivity, through medicine and other physical modalities that support our health.

Sickness is one of the most painful crucifixions we experi-

crucifixions we experience as humans. Prayer and meditation are powerful tools in the prevention of disease, as well as the amelioration of its effects, because they lift the mind above the body. The body heals best when we're not looking at it* (T-401). As our minds rise to a realm above the body, the body has more of a chance to relax and restore itself. We should treat the body with great gratitude and respect, for it is a priceless material gift. But the body is not who we are.

MEDITATION FOR PHYSICAL WELLNESS

Close your eyes and see yourself lying on a flat white marble slab in front of Jesus.

See him as he lifts his hands above you.

See the emanation of a great light pouring forth from his hands and covering your body, then entering into it.

Watch the light as its power is concentrated on any wound or wounded area in your body.

Allow the light from his hands to move through your blood, restoring every cell, every organ, every muscle, every bone.

Continuing to relax, breathing deeply, surrender your body to the Holy Spirit. Ask that He use your hands, your feet, every aspect of your physical self to aid Him in His healing of the world.

Hold this meditation for at least two minutes, a minimum of five if possible.

If done daily, this meditation will do you extraordinary good.

Death

I have a friend who had a near-death experience due to anaphylactic shock, in which she was looking down on her body and heard the doctor say, "We lost her." In the realm to which she was delivered during that experience, she saw clearly that her body was not her real Self. Others have reported similar instances of near-death experience, commonly reporting that they lost all fear of death because they know that they lived through it.

The life of the body is precious, and nothing in the teaching of the *Course* minimizes its magnificence. It is a beautiful lesson in communion. The message of the *Course* is not that the body is bad, but that in a way it is nothing. All our tribulations in life are due to an attachment and overidentification with the life of the body. In truth, we have the most powerful, meaningful, and joyful experience of the body when we know that it is not who we are.

As I write this I am nearing my seventieth birthday, as shocked as I'm sure everyone is when they find themselves facing that particular milestone. All of us carry around a secret hope that somehow age will not apply to us. I remember it wasn't until I was about twenty-five that it seriously dawned on me that, yes, I too would one day die.

Carl Jung said that a failure to deal with the subject of death robs the second half of life of its meaning. I can see where that's true. I'm surprised by people who are aging with what seems to be a prejudice against talking about death, as though if we ignore it, it will magically disappear. I don't know how anyone is handling all the chaos in the world today without a spiritual connection. I certainly can't understand how anyone faces death without one.

Given that the spirit is eternal, death is like taking off a suit of clothes. Knowing there is a truer truth than the one we perceive with our physical senses, the idea of no longer perceiving with those senses is not all that frightening a thought. The message of Jesus is that in reality there is no death.

I'm at an age where a lot of people who have been closest to me have passed through the veil of death. They now seem to be standing on the other side of it gazing into my soul as I am gazing into theirs. And having been present at many deathbeds, both personally and professionally, I have seen the power of life overwhelm the fear of death, so great was the love that was present.

According to *A Course in Miracles*, one day death will be seen not as the punishment, but as the reward for a life well lived. The light we see around each other will be so great that the body itself will appear as mere shadow, and the removal of the shadow will mean nothing more than the removal of a belief in limits. To say death shall be the last enemy is to say that one day we will see that it simply isn't an enemy, for in truth it doesn't exist.

The only real death is the death of love, and we triumph over that in any moment when we choose love instead of fear. Jesus has demonstrated that death does not exist, and in any moment when we rise as he rose we share in his resurrection and increase its blessing on all the world.

MEDITATION ON DEATH

Dear God,
We surrender the soul of our beloved _____ to You.
May he (or she) be lifted gently into the regions of heaven.
May those of us still here be comforted in our grief.
We see a golden cord that ties the heart of one who has passed
to the heart of those still here who love them.
We see Jesus as he puts his hands upon this cord,
thus we see the eternal nature of life and love.
For whom God hath brought together,
nothing, not even death itself,
can put asunder.
And so it is.
So great is God.
Amen

The Crucified World

We are living in a crucified world, humanity hanging on a cross of our own making. With our attachment to the illusions of separation, our mental imprisonment by thoughts of fear, our constant attacks on ourselves and each other, our planet is teetering on the brink of destruction.

The message of the crucifixion is that this need not be. Children don't have to be committing suicide in an effort to escape the pain of adolescence; people don't have to be drowning themselves in drugs and alcohol to avoid the pain of surviving; countries don't need to be spending more of their resources on ways to kill each other than on ways to heal each other; and the health of the planet doesn't have to decline precipitously under the weight of our greed and exploitation. *None of this need be.*

It is our mindset, our worldview, our thought system that has created the hell we're enduring and that so threatens our future. But for the world to change, *we* must be willing to change. We must be willing to put everything on the altar; all that we are, all that we have, and all that we do must be brought up for review. We cannot bring the light to the darkness; we must bring our darkness to the light.

If we remain the same, then so will the world. And the world is moving in a direction that does not produce hope. Hope is born of hopeful solutions, and the only real hopeful solution is that we be willing to love each other as God so loves us.

As we do, a field of possibility will open up before us— miraculous in scope, historic in nature, summing up all the hopes and all the dreams of a world that now seems so bound.

CHAPTER FIVE

RESURRECTION

Very simply, the resurrection is the overcoming or surmounting of death. It is a reawakening or a rebirth; a change of mind about the meaning of the world. It is the acceptance of the Holy Spirit's interpretation of the world's purpose; the acceptance of the Atonement for oneself. It is the end of dreams of misery, and the glad awareness of the Holy Spirit's final dream. It is the recognition of the gifts of God. It is the dream in which the body functions perfectly, having no function except communication. It is the lesson in which learning ends, for it is consummated and surpassed with this. It is the invitation to God to take His final step. It is the relinquishment of all other purposes, all other interests, all other wishes and all other concerns. It is the single desire of the Son for the Father.* (MT-68)

A T THIS HISTORIC time of phase transition, an entire era of human history is passing away. What this period will be replaced by is completely up to us: things will either get very dark or very light. Accumulated layers of fear—evidenced politically, economically, and socially—have now reached a point where they will destroy us if we do not intervene on our own behalf.

While free will is always operative, there is a limit beyond which our wrong-minded attitudes and behavior simply become unworkable. We are called upon now to be both death doulas to a world that is no longer working and birth doulas to a world that is struggling to be born. Nothing less than fundamental pattern disruption will lead to a sustainable future.

Many are diagnosed today with an "anxiety disorder." An anxiety disorder isn't just an individual's diagnosis, however; it's the state of the world today. Looking at this only as an individual's problem distracts us from the larger issue of spiritual suffering, not just on the part of an individual but on the part of our society.

All of us are influenced by the fear-based thinking of the world, but seeing ourselves as victims of it only perpetuates the insanity. The world is saturated by the ego's malignant mentality, and without the medicine of spiritual understanding, it easily crawls into our psyche.

There's nothing new there. We know what the ego has to say; now it's time for the ego to hear what *we* have to say. Crucifixion alludes to our madness, and the resurrection is the return of sanity. It is a change of heart among us so powerful that the world itself will be transformed.

The world we live in today *is* an anxiety disorder, for the very reason that love does not guide the world. It is not the organizing principle for our civilization. The ego's thought system is allowed to run roughshod over the human heart, a constant generator of fear and anxiety, and the only solution to the problem is the dismantling of this thought system. Jesus is a model for and guide to right-minded thinking, sending ego thoughts back to the nothingness whence they came.

I have asked audiences around the country if anyone in the

room had either said, or heard a young person say, that under normal circumstances they would consider having children but that the state of the world today makes them hesitate. In every audience, a significant number of people raised their hand. This should not be considered normal. Perhaps if we face the malfunctioning of the world we have made for ourselves, we might consider whether God has a better way.

Millions of people, perhaps more, have held Jesus at bay because of the traditional religious constructs that have grown up around him. But as we take an evolutionary stride toward an enlightened view of the world, we are beginning to see him with new eyes. His resurrection is not just some theological dogma. It is the activation of new life within us.

The mind when unaligned with God is the cause of all suffering; the mind when aligned with Him is the cause of suffering's end. Jesus is a portal to a field of unspeakable love and power. Yet the portal means nothing if we don't walk through it. The aspiration of the miracle worker is to lift our consciousness so close to God's that we become masters, not slaves, of the mortal world.

We gaze into the eyes of Jesus that he might show us another world.

The Alchemy of Easter

Such is your resurrection, for your life is not a part of anything you see. It stands beyond the body and the world, past every witness for unholiness, within the Holy, holy as Itself. (WB-279)

The meaning of Easter is what happens in any moment when love and forgiveness overcome the fear-laden powers of the world.

There's an obvious intensification on the planet now of both darkness and light, both forces of planetary destruction and planetary enlightenment. The question of how to break the chain of darkness could not be more relevant than it is today. Environmental degradation, rising authoritarianism, and endless war are the stuff of our collective crucifixion. The air is so saturated with toxicity now that our minds, our bodies, our entire civilization is feeling the dis-ease. Even those of faith, of serious and committed spiritual practice, are having to work overtime to keep a creeping despair at bay.

Humanity can't stop the madness, because humanity *is* the madness. What is needed on the planet now is a collective resurrection, a divine intercession from a thought system beyond our own.

So what will happen now? Will darkness and fear, or light and love, win the struggle for the future? If we simply give up and surrender, darkness most certainly will win. But if we stand up and fight back, then darkness might also win. As long as we fight, then we're stuck in the fight. Is there any other option?

Interestingly enough, yes. The other option is resurrection, the evolution of the human race.

This isn't just about Jesus; it's about us. Resurrection two thousand years ago was an overcoming by one man; resurrection today is an overcoming by each of us, and by the entire species. We ourselves must become the change, and *that* is the resurrection. God cannot do for us that which He cannot do through us. We must be willing to be reborn into a higher version of ourselves if we're to achieve the miracle of planetary transformation. The world as it now exists is a reflection of who we have been; the world of the future will reflect who we choose to become. We can have the overcoming, but not if we hang on to the cross.

Whether it be our attachment to the past, or to our addictions, or to our judgments, or to our victimization, or to our violent behavior—we can have those, or we can have a survivable future. Only if we work to rid the darkness from our own hearts can we become the conduits of miraculous change.

The resurrection is the revelation of God's eternal imprint on every moment, in every life. It is the potential for light that exists within even the deepest darkness. It is the reason to hope when all hope seems lost. It is the possibility for a new beginning that seems impossible when all has gone wrong. As a principle, resurrection does not require our recognition to exist. But as a practical reality, it requires our willingness to become fully activated in human affairs. Salvation begins when we consider the possibility that there might be better way* (T-22). This opens the mind to divine illumination, to a new kind of experience we become less and less willing to deny.

At Easter, we celebrate our ability to rise above the consciousness of darkness, ignorance, and death. Something begins to change within us; our openness to the deeper meaning of the resurrection opens doors within the heart. Jesus died, and then he rose. Now it's our turn.

We too can radically transform. The crucified self can be transmuted and turned to light. On this day, may we each rediscover at the deepest level the meaning of "Hallelujah" and the reason to praise God.

In the words of the *Course*, "Let us not spend this holy week brooding on the crucifixion of God's Son, but happily in the celebration of his *release*. For Easter is the sign of peace, not pain"* (T-425).

The resurrection is a description of how the universe operates, how it self-corrects, how life always reasserts itself even when forces of death and darkness have temporarily prevailed. Like a tiny flower growing through cracks in broken cement, peace of mind can emerge at last after periods of grief have ravaged the heart, and people can fall in love despite having experienced the cruelest predicaments. Time and time again, love reappears after even the most crushing events. To embrace the resurrection means to recognize what's true; it's the way of the universe that God will always have the final say.

That is why we cleave to God; because we want to transform our own circumstances and find victory in our own lives. Spiritual realization affects us physically, emotionally, and psychologically because it reorients our relationship to the universe. It reorients our sense of self as well as our relationship to others. The last thing the spiritual journey does is to distract us from the practical realities of life. By understanding the underlying meaning of our life's journey, we gain power to direct and to redirect its course. Knowing we are not *of* this world gives us more power within it.

The Messiah is a state of mind, the unconditional love that is a conduit for our enlightenment. The question isn't simply what we need to do; the question is what quality of personhood we must embody in order to do what we are asked to do. All of us are being asked right now. In each of our lives there is some circumstance challenging us to give up a weaker part of ourselves and emerge into a stronger place. All of us are wounded by this world, but it's our choice whether or not to act from the wound. In acting from the wound, we perpetuate a wounded world. In choosing to transcend the wound, we'll create a world reborn.

Jesus wasn't putting on some macabre show for the world to witness; he was changing the molecular structure of the universe. He was opening up possibilities for change not only for himself but for all the world. Even those of us who do not relate to his story as Christians can relate to the metaphysical power of the resurrection and to its transformative effect upon our lives. Any one person breaking the hold of darkness paves the way for everyone to break the hold of darkness.

And then there is Light.

The Remembrance

The resurrection is the remembrance of who we are.

While we've been trained by the ego's thought system to believe we're limited, temporary, vulnerable beings within a world of scarcity, in competition with most everyone and everything, the mystic Jesus means we are none of those things. We remain who and what God created us to be, despite any evidence of the material world. No illusion of our guilt, no disapproval of the world, no mistakes we have made or lies of the earthly realm can in any way change or nullify the truth as God created it.

Whatever our suffering, and whatever its cause, our deliverance from pain derives from a reinterpretation of reality. Jesus delivers us beyond our emotional pain by delivering us beyond our mental errors. It is simply an error in thinking to believe that anything has more power than God. We can be hurt, wronged, transgressed against, even killed—but the truth of who we are is not vulnerable to the machinations of the ego, whether our own or someone else's. God's Truth is the only Truth. The truth of who we are cannot be hurt and cannot die. As long as our hearts are open to love—as long as we remember we are one with God—we are miraculously delivered from the ravages of our crucifixions as Jesus was delivered from his.

The point of the crucifixion is not the suffering of Jesus; the point is the resurrection that followed. The crucifixion was an extreme example of the ego's attack on love. The resurrection was God's response to the crucifixion, or the ultimate reappearance of the light after even the deepest darkness. Having lived through the journey of the deepest darkness to the most glorious light, Jesus looks not for martyrs but for teachers to demonstrate that same power.

We are asked to share in the power of his resurrection now, to bestow its healing on the world in ways that he directs. We become transformers of the darkness of the world as we are resurrected from our own crucifixions. God works miracles for us that we might become miracle workers ourselves.

Jesus suffered and then resurrected to demonstrate the spiritual nullification of suffering. If you or I are going through a terrible time, let's say we've been wronged somehow, and Jesus guides us to forgive—telling us that infinite love will work a miracle in the situation—then had he not been crucified and resurrected, would we not wonder, *But how would you know?* And if a loved one dies and we're grieving—and Jesus tells us not to be sorrowful, because the death of their body is not the death of who they are—then had he not been crucified and resurrected, would we not wonder, *But how can you be sure?*

Delving into the mysteries of any hero's journey can unlock secrets otherwise unavailable to our conscious mind. The crucifixion and resurrection of Jesus are among the deepest of mysteries. Where parts of us have died, God brings our deadened places to new life. He restores the cosmic order to situations where even the most horrifying chaos reigned before. Human suffering is inevitable in a world that is permeated with illusion and fear, yet through the power of forgiveness we can and do transform it. With every prayer, every moment of faith, every act of mercy, every instant of contrition, every effort at forgiveness, in time we move beyond our suffering and find inner peace at last.

We die to who we used to be and are reborn as who we are, thus rising above the consciousness of darkness, ignorance, and death. Each of us goes through this repeatedly—we all have our own curriculum, our own crucifixions, our own battles and trials and tribulations. But each of us has within us as well the potential for enlightenment and resurrection, as an indwelling God Who both calls us out of darkness and delivers us to light.

There is a lot of talk in our culture today that glorifies the darkness. Mentally as well as physically, we pick apart our problems and dissect their every vicissitude. But as important as it is to own our darkness, we should also own our light. Jesus is a name for that light. We should not be mesmerized by the crucifixion. Understand the darkness, but look beyond it to the light.

The resurrected mind is the light of God within us. It is the mind that understands. It understands that only love is real, and nothing else exists. It understands that illusions dissolve in the presence of love. It understands that the power to transform the world lies in our power to think about it differently. Understanding anew, we become new. We are not just improved; we are *changed.*

Three days after the crucifixion of Jesus, the women who were closest to him went to the tomb to claim his body. A great earthquake occurred, and they were told he was no longer there. "Why do you look for the living among the dead? He isn't here, but has been raised" (Luke 24:5-6, CEB). Once you've survived a personal crucifixion and been resurrected into a higher level of understanding, the part of your personality that was crucified by the event no longer exists. That person has been transmuted into who you are now. You no longer have certain issues, are no longer stuck in certain patterns of thought and behavior, are no longer blinded by self, are no longer chained to the cross of your own self-destructive ego. An internal earthquake indeed.

In psychological terms, the resurrection isn't so much an event as a process. It is both an awakening and a journey, as we emerge from the torment of facing our own internal demons into the light of having faced them down. And the benefits of the journey are cumulative. We become different because of what we've been through. We become wiser, nobler, more humble, and more aware. We become more peaceful and more open to the miracles of life. The holiest work of all is finding this wholeness within, where all the broken pieces of our selves have converged in forgiveness and love. That wholeness is our holiness. Such is the miracle of redemption: transformation and rebirth.

Having been "saved" from ego consciousness, Jesus now has a role of savior to those of us still lost within it. And lost we are, while we're suffering the illusions of the ego mind. Jesus is someone who, his mind having been completely healed by the Holy Spirit, has been authorized by God to help anyone who calls to him to do the same. Jesus's mind, joined with our mind, can shine away the ego.

This takes more than "believing in him," however. It takes joining with him in miracle-minded thoughts that are the escape from our mortal hell. The "belief" in God is ultimately meaningless if not matched by lived experience. According to *A Course in Miracles*, many conspire with God who do not yet believe in Him. Where there is love, He is there. Where there is not love, He is not fooled.

It is we who have been fooled. The world of illusion–backed as it is by a wall of dense material reality–can be as powerful in its effects as is the truth. But we are beginning to see beyond it. The mortal world is a dream within which it is our spiritual task to awaken. Resurrection is our awakening, for it dissolves the dark illusion of a separated self by embracing the light of forgiveness and love. God *is* the Light, and in cleaving to the light we become transformers of the dark. In darkness, there is only war and death; in light, there is peace on earth and good will to one another.

If God Is in the Cockpit

Jesus lived as a man, yes, and was the full manifestation or embodiment of the Holy Spirit. That is amazing and awe-inspiring. But it is no less amazing that he lives within us now, no longer embodied but still alive. He lives in another realm of consciousness and we can meet him there.

The crucifixion was the last useless journey into fear, the final demonstration that the power of love overcomes all other. The message of the resurrection is that in the presence of love, the ego has no power. The truth of who you are cannot be crucified.

The insults we relate to that need not affect us, the memories we hang on to that need not torment us, the things we fear that we need not even think about—think how different your life will be when you're no longer held back by the fearful dramas of this world. The ego has assigned to us the life of a slave, imprisoned within a tiny cell of our own making, crouching within it and unable to spread either arms or legs, much less grow wings.

The resurrection is the realization that this need not be. If others lied about you, it doesn't matter. If you failed at something in your past, you can let it go and be more successful now.

If someone doesn't want to be with you any longer, the form of the relationship has changed but the love that was ever there lives on. That is what it means to grow our wings. It means we fly above the illusions of this world, to heights from which we can be more effective at helping others to be released from theirs.

This isn't abstract, it's practical. It is the transition from chronic stress to inner peace. Whenever someone tells me God is their co-pilot, I laugh. If God's in the cockpit, as far as I'm concerned He can take the wheel.

We can step back and let God lead the way* (WB-291). We can surrender all we have and all we are, asking to be used for a higher purpose than our own.

We are asked to be His hands and feet; we are the faucets, we're not the water. The awesome power of God is within us but not of us. We're not its source; we're its conduits. Think of the universe as wired for the electricity of God. All of us are lamps. It doesn't matter the shape of the lamp, the design of the lamp, or how old the lamp is. What matters is whether or not the lamp is plugged in.

With every prayer, we plug in. With every moment of forgiveness, we plug in. With every "Jesus, you take this," we plug in. He is the heart's intelligence, far greater than our own.

Our spiritual liberation doesn't lie in bursting out but in melting in. Our gentleness is stronger than our harshness, our humility is stronger than our arrogance, and our flexibility is stronger than our self-will.

Where there is love there cannot be fear. When the mind summons Jesus, fear subsides. You literally feel a difference in the energy of your body when an issue is given over to the intelligence of the heart. Nervousness is replaced by inner peace.

I have felt this personally. Having both succeeded and failed at various things in my life, I've had a lot of time to think about the differences.

Where I failed, I see that I walked ahead of the truth. I thought I had to figure everything out. I tried to exert my self-will. I walked ahead of God.

Where I succeeded, I surrendered to something greater than myself, not as an act of obedience but as an act of power. I remembered that of myself I'm just one person challenged by powers much greater than mine; in service to him, I'm aligned with a power beyond the powers of the world.

Looking at the world today, one realizes that, as they say in Alcoholics Anonymous, our best thinking got us here. And as Einstein made clear, the thinking that got us here is not the thinking that will lead us out of here.

That is why there is a spiritual revival on the planet today. It's why so many are ready to humble ourselves before a power greater than our own, a power that can do for us what we cannot do for ourselves.

There is a way. There is a door to a world we want, a world of peace where we are free to love and to be loved. There are many names on the door, and one of them is Jesus. If when you look at the door you see his name, he is ready to swing it open in any moment that you say yes.

Put out your hand, and see how easily the door swings open with your one intent to go beyond it. Angels light the way, so that all darkness vanishes, and you are standing in a light so bright and clear that you can understand all things you see. A tiny moment of surprise, perhaps, will

make you pause before you realize the world you see before
you in the light reflects the truth you knew, and did not
quite forget in wandering away in dreams.* (W-131)

IMAGINE JESUS

Sit comfortably and imagine Jesus living within you. Literally melt into his energy and allow his to melt into yours. Breathe in his being.

Stay with that visualization for a minimum of five minutes, if you can...

As you walk around today, remember that he is closer than your breath to you. With every conscious thought that he is there, dysfunctional energies dissolve and melt away. They go back to the nothingness whence they came.

Dear God,
Please do for me what I cannot do for myself.
Overrule the darkness and fill me with Your Light.
Help me to see the innocence in everyone.
Lift my soul
and renew my body.
Open my eyes that I might see
the love that is always there.
Amen

He Did Not Ignore

How does the entire world evolve or get saved from the catastrophe of our collective self-destruction? It's lovely to think that we as individuals can heal our thoughts and thus change our lives. But isn't there more at stake than just your salvation or mine? In an age of constant wars, environmental degradation, and all manner of other global disasters, are we not challenged collectively to spiritually evolve?

Resurrection is a new sensibility arising on the earth today. It is brought about by those who sense that there is another world possible and who know in their deepest being that it's our purpose to bring it forth. This is not a religious perspective, although it is a sacred one. People from all religions, and no religions, are awakening to the truth of the heart today.

Humanity is giving birth to a new historical era. Labor happens when it happens, but the laboring mother still has to push. The creation of a new world is not always easy, and it is rarely appreciated by the protectors of the old. Jesus is a mystical aid to both directing and enduring the process.

From our collective resurrection will emerge a transformed world. It will still be a dream compared to God's ultimate reality, but a happy dream from which awakening occurs more naturally* (T-383). There will be no war, no poverty, no needless suffering. Humanity having remembered its identity and purpose, the world will be a different place. Form will be secondary to the primacy of spirit.

Our consciousness rising, unimportant things will mean less to us. The arc of evolution is bending in the direction of justice, and we were born to be its benders. Even if we are so irresponsible as to manifest global catastrophe, and there are only a very few people left on the planet at the end of that, those few will look at each other and say, "This time let's do things differently."

The mystic is led by the heart, yes. But seeing the body through a spiritual lens, we gain more physical life force with which to do the heart's bidding. The mystic's life is one of neither physical nor intellectual laziness. It is not a life of negative denial regarding the problems of the world. The aspirant doesn't say that since only love is real and everything else is an illusion anyway, there's nothing for us to do except to try to heal our own lives. There is no spiritual justification for ignoring the suffering of the world. The fact that something is happening within a realm of illusion doesn't mean it doesn't matter. Jesus wept; he did not ignore.

Jesus doesn't ignore the hungry; he feeds the hungry. He doesn't just talk about peace; he wages peace. He doesn't demonize the poor; he helps them. All those things will take a miracle, given the ego-driven institutional resistance to letting such values lead. But he is with us to provide those miracles. Miracles don't seem unreasonable when you know they occur naturally as expressions of love.

The Mountain

Jesus proclaimed, "Repent, for the kingdom of heaven has come near." "On earth as it is in heaven" means on the material plane as we know it should be in our hearts.

It's now time for *us* to repent–to think again–to atone for what was wrong in the past and imagine what is possible. A new world is at hand, if we are willing to rethink the one we are living in now.

The life of the miracle worker isn't just determined by what we do but by who we are. Having reached a more peaceful, centered place within our consciousness, the point then becomes what to do with who we have become.

Jesus called forth the menders of nets, which means people with the right skill sets to help you. He made his disciples fishermen of men, which means he will make you a leader–someone who demonstrates how to build communities based on strong human values. He healed disease and cured the sickness of a wounded world; he will show you how to use your energies for the same kind of purposes in our world today.

As people began to harken to his words, Jesus went up to the mountain. Just as Moses was called to Mount Nebo, just as Mary was called to the roof, all of us are called to the higher place– the realms of meditation and prayer–for only there are we able to hear, to think, to understand in deeper and higher ways. The more God's power heals your life, the *more* you want to pray, the *more* you want to meditate, the *more* you want to remember to give your life to God.

The point of your life is that it be used as a platform from which to help heal the world. Jesus saw the crowds, and so will you. He sat down, which should remind you to ground yourself. His disciples came to him, and you too will be joined by like-minded souls. And he began to speak.

You too will now be led to take action.

No matter what form your activity takes, it can be your ministry. It can be the way you help improve your corner of the world. It is the spirit of contribution you put into your work that makes it meaningful—not so much its form as its content. What's important is that we do whatever we do as a way of serving love.

The Holy Spirit knows exactly who you are and what you've been through. He will tell you exactly where to go and what to do. Your successes as well as your failures are all of equal value to Him in healing the world, as long as you are willing to be used as a conduit for His love. The only real failure is something we failed to learn from. It is our willingness to be used by Him now that determines our spiritual value as agents of healing.

Jesus is said to have told his disciples to go out into the countryside and teach the gospel. To teach is to demonstrate, and the gospel is love. He wasn't telling his disciples to go out and hit people over the head with their book. Nor is he saying that to his disciples today. He is telling us to teach love and love only, for love is what we are. The disciple isn't trying to get his message out; we're trying to get his message *in*. It's our inner ear into which he whispers and reveals all things.

The ego plays a zero-sum game, telling you that what you give away you lose. But on a spiritual plane, you get to keep only what you give away. Jesus was able to multiply the loaves and fishes because he needed them to feed people. When you live only to feed people in one way or another, all material abundance you need to support the task will be provided to you as well.

We ask to be guided by Him, and used by Him, to play whatever role we might best play in His plan for the healing of the world. We can't see the whole picture or where we would best fit in, but if we make ourselves available, God Himself will take us up on our offer. We'll be directed to where we might be most helpful. He has perfect faith in us to accomplish every task on which we are sent, and He will offer us His faith in place of our doubts.

> *There is a way of living in the world that is not here, although it seems to be. You do not change appearance, though you smile more frequently. Your forehead is serene; your eyes are quiet. And the ones who walk the world as you do recognize their own. Yet those who have not yet perceived the way will recognize you also, and believe that you are like them, as you were before.* (WB-291)*

His disciples represent the presence of an Alternative—a more merciful, compassionate, and forgiving way of being—in a personal relationship, a business setting, or even world affairs.

The resurrection is not a life of sacrifice but a life of joy. It doesn't mean dying for humanity but living for humanity. The only thing we "sacrifice" are parts of ourselves we come to see were self-sabotaging, double-edged swords to begin with. We sacrifice being judgmental, we sacrifice being cowardly, we sacrifice being negative, we sacrifice playing small. Those are the things we allow to die so that God within us may live.

Awakening from the Dream

Your Friend goes with you. You are not alone. No one who calls on Him can call in vain. Whatever troubles you, be certain that He has the answer, and will gladly give it to you, if you simply turn to Him and ask it of Him. He will not withhold all answers that you need for anything that seems to trouble you. He knows the way to solve all problems, and resolve all doubts. His certainty is yours. You need but ask it of Him, and it will be given you.* (WB-Epilogue)

The ego is the mind of separation, and as long as we're living in this world we will always be prone to think in terms of separate bodies rather than unified spirits. But it's possible to live in this world, even be deeply grounded in the blessings of this world, yet see the purpose of every day, and every interaction, as being a lesson in becoming a more loving human being.

We need to own our errors and be willing to correct them. We need to acknowledge our defects and surrender them for healing. We need to be willing to see we're no better or worse than anyone else. We need to be willing to step back and let the Holy Spirit lead the way, replacing our self-will with His higher wisdom and knowledge of all things. We need to be willing to dwell in the present, to let the past go. We need to be willing to see that only love is real and everything else is illusion.

The world is in a state of spiritual slumber. There has never been a mass awakening but it's time for one, for in our sleep the nightmares have come and they are threatening to destroy the world.

We do not go directly, however, from a state of sleep to a state of awakening. Jesus helps us translate the painful dream we're in now to a happy dream, a world in which hunger and poverty and war shall be no more. "And God Himself shall wipe away all tears"* (WB-450).

The world we live in is but a reflection of the people we have been. Our neglect, even disavowal, of the sacred has led us to where we are. Our lack of reverence and devotion, for God, for the planet, for each other, and even for ourselves, is the cause of our individual and collective pain.

But God, being perfect Love, has an answer to every problem the moment the problem occurs. That applies collectively as well as individually. God's response to the challenges the world faces today is a collective plan for the world's redemption. Through it, each of us is infused with the wisdom to play the role we best might play in the healing of the world.

The plan works within the world much the way our immune system works within the body. Cells are sent to the wound in order to heal it, and we, as healers, are similarly sent to heal the wounds of society. As cells in the body might be assigned to the pancreas, or the liver, or the blood, we will be assigned to the arts, to education, to business, or to any other area where we can be of greatest service. We will know what work is ours to do because we will feel a quickening that informs us. Some endeavors, such as politics, are a collective assignment. We are sent to where we can be most helpful.

By allowing Jesus to guide our thinking, we are allowing him to guide our lives. With our rational, mortal mind we do not know what's going to happen tomorrow, nor how our path fits into the larger scheme of things. But the Holy Spirit does. The greatest way to serve the unfoldment of the best possible tomorrow is by settling as deeply as possible into love and forgiveness today.

"Heaven and earth shall be as one" means the day will come when they will no longer exist as two separate states. Our thoughts will be purified of fear, so our planet will be purified of fear as well. That is our destiny; we will get there through wisdom or we will get there through pain. How long it will take, and how much suffering we will have to go through first, is entirely up to us. But our healing is foreordained, because God's Will has never not been done. "If I am with you in the loneliness of the world, the loneliness is gone"* (T-144).

I have borne witness to much agony in my life. I have sat at many deathbeds. I have held parents in my arms who just saw their child take their last breath. I have seen, and I have experienced, the torture of heartbreak. Yet in the lives of others, as in my own life as well, I have seen deep darkness turn into light. I have seen hope again in the eyes of those who formerly had none. I have seen how the universe operates. I have seen the glory of God.

We came from love and shall return to love. There is no question this will happen after we die, but the bigger point is, we can go there now. We don't have to wait until death to experience the deathless. Our eyes can be reopened, right here, right now.

Where the mystic Jesus is made welcome, there he is.

ACKNOWLEDGMENTS

Writing is very private, but it can take a lot of people to make a writer's work possible. I am deeply grateful to the people who have done this for me.

Thank you from the bottom of my heart...

To Andrea Cagan, who once again became my muse when the words were in me but I couldn't find them.

To Robert Perry, who generously lent me his brilliance and insight into *A Course in Miracles*.

To Emily Bennington, whose gracious work with Robert at the Circle of Atonement lent insight and direction.

To Lauren Selsky, Cathy Parr, Cindy Alvarado, Gina Vucci, Debo Grim, and Tammy Brenizer, for handling with excellence and grace the world that swirled around me as I wrote.

To Ellis Levine, for continuing to guide my publishing career.

To Tammy Vogsland, for making sure my world didn't fall apart as I wrote.

To Gabriella Page-Fort, who showed great care and generosity in bringing the book to completion.

To assistant editor Ryan Amato, production editor Lisa Zuniga, copyeditor Cathy Cambron, interior designer Leah Carlson-Stanisic, interior design manager Yvonne Chan, and cover designer Stephen Brayda. To marketer Julia Kent, publicists

Courtney Nobile and Alison Cerri, deputy publisher Laina Adler, and publisher Judith Curr. Thanks to all of you for doing such a wonderful job.

To my daughter, India, my greatest blessing.

And to Mickey Maudlin for the years of wise direction, for giving me the chance to write this book, and believing that I could.

ABOUT THE AUTHOR

MARIANNE WILLIAMSON is an internationally acclaimed lecturer and *New York Times* bestselling author with fourteen published books, including *A Return to Love*. She has been a popular guest on a number of television programs, including *Oprah*, *Larry King Live*, *Good Morning America*, and *Charlie Rose*. Williamson is the founder of Project Angel Food, a meals-on-wheels program that serves homebound people with AIDS in the Los Angeles area. She is a native of Houston, Texas.